Fatherland

BY JOHANNA MOORE BAXANDALL

Translated from the German
by
Robert Alston Jones and Beth Lee Weckmueller,
with
Foreword and Afterword by Melanie Moore Steen

DORRANCE PUBLISHING CO
EST. 1920
PITTSBURGH, PENNSYLVANIA 15238

Dorrance Publishing Co
585 Alpha Drive
Pittsburgh, PA 15238
Visit our website at *www.dorrancebookstore.com*

ISBN: 978-1-6495-7148-9
eISBN: 978-1-6495-7657-6

Foreword

This is my mother's story. She is the "Christina" who narrates what follows. Born in Germany in 1928, she came to the US as a "war bride" in 1948, shortly after marrying my American father, a US Army officer. While there is no shortage of narratives by women whose lives changed dramatically when they came to the United States as brides of US soldiers returning home, most of these relate their accommodation to their new environments and experiences after leaving their native homelands. Far fewer record their lives before they assumed new identities in marriages that took them away from the familiar into the unknown.

The typewritten memoir about my mother's life prior to her marriage was discovered only after her death. Precisely when she wrote her story is not known, although it is likely that she was in her late sixties. Whenever it was that she undertook to construct this story of her early life, I believe she had decided that it was important—for both herself and others—to give an account of her experiences as a child, teenager, and young woman growing up in the Germany of the Third Reich, and to explain how those years had molded her into the individual she had become.

Although she changed some of the names among the cast of characters, my mother crafted her story from the memories of her relationships with her parents and other family members, as well as with classmates and other friends. Instead of constructing a diaristic, first-person narrative, she writes from a third-person perspective, interpreting her own biography up to her marriage and subsequent departure from her "fatherland" (both country and parent) while attempting to articulate the complexities and traumas of growing up in Germany during the years chronicled here. As she interprets her memories, she brings to the surface deep-seated feelings about herself and her past. She tries to make sense of who she was then relative to who she is now, and what her early life might mean for her not-yet-experienced future. Her story is a reconstruction purposefully authored to reveal both what she then knew and experienced, as well as give voice to a history that would elucidate for others the character of the individual they think they know.

My mother's review of her life up to her marriage is not recorded as simple reportage but is consciously crafted with the literary devices of wit, humor, sarcasm, irony, and vivid imagery. Her story, written in German and in a style that reveals my mother's personality in every sentence, has been translated by two of her close friends and former colleagues, Beth Lee Weckmueller and Robert Alston Jones. Whether read in the original German or in this translation, this account of my mother's early life distils the essence of her character and illuminates the temper of the times that shaped her.

Melanie Moore Steen
July 2020

Translators' Notes to the Reader

The memoir references members of the author's extended family. The main characters are the following:

- Christina Steiger, the person whose story is told in *Fatherland*. As the story begins, she is the person referred to as "the mother" of an unnamed daughter whose curiosity about her mother's earlier life in Germany triggers the author's account of her childhood and young adulthood.
- Elise (Elizabeth) Steiger, Christina's mother.
- Philipp Steiger, Christina's father, an architect and builder, an avowed Communist.
- Mr. Morey/Matt, the American army officer Christina marries.

Christina's maternal relatives are:

- Oma Stina (aka "Stina"), Christina Berry, Christina's maternal grandmother and namesake.
- Opa (Peter) Berry, Christina's maternal grandfather.
- Tante Lisa, Elise's sister and her closest confidante. Tante Lisa's husband is Onkel Werner.

- Ernst August, Christina's first cousin, son of Tante Lisa and Onkel Werner.
- Tante Anna, Elise's sister, married to Onkel Karl.
- Karl and Georg, Christina's first cousins, sons of Tante Anna and Onkel Karl.
- Tante Käthe, Elise's youngest sister.
- Tante Klara, Elise's sister.
- Tina, Christina's first cousin, daughter of Tante Klara.
- Onkel Peter, Elise's brother.
- Tante Rosa, Elise's sister married to Onkel Robert.
- Tante Susanne, Elise's sister.
- Tilde, Christina's first cousin, daughter of Tante Susanne.
- Marie, Elise's sister.

Christina's paternal relatives are:

- Margarethe, née Steiger (aka "Tall Gret," "Tante Greta"). Philipp Steiger's eldest sister.
- Karl, husband of Tante Greta (a second Onkel Karl).
- Onkel Adam, Philipp's brother.
- Tante Eva, Philipp's elder sister who raised him after their mother died in childbirth. Her husband is Onkel Thomas.
- Hans and Liesl, Christina's first cousins, children of Tante Eva and Onkel Thomas.
- Kurt and Heinz, foster children raised by Tante Eva.
- Onkel Seppel (also "Sepp," [nickname for Joseph]), Philipp's brother, married to Erna, née Wagner.

German has been retained for the following:

- Herr = Mr.
- Frau = Mrs.

- Fräulein = Miss (American soldiers tended to pronounce this as "Frollein"—as it appears twice in the text.)
- Tante = Aunt
- Onkel = Uncle
- Oma = Grandma
- Opa = Grandpa
- Strasse = street, e.g. Hindenburgstrasse = Hindenburg Street
- Amis = Americans, a common term for American soldiers

Fatherland

She was different, this mother. Her daughter learned this from her playmates, who compared her to their own mothers.

She walked differently, usually barefoot, skirt hiked up, as though she were striding through a meadow instead of across the manicured lawn in front of her modest California ranch house.

And that was all fine for a while—until the daughter started hearing things about this foreign country that were worse than she could have imagined.

There must have been times when she thought about this a lot; a child doesn't come up with questions like "Did you get to play there?" out of the blue. A question like this requires imagining a place where playing might not be allowed.

The daughter began avoiding the word "Nazi" once she learned it meant the same thing as "German." Clearly her mother was not a Nazi, since there was not a single picture of her in a uniform in the album of photos documenting her mother's earlier life. Nazis didn't wear dirndls and straw hats—she was sure of that.

But then something happened that completely changed the way she thought about the place her mother came from. She saw the movie about Anne Frank. And she could not imagine how that could have happened.

"How could you all?"

The time had come. The usual evasive maneuvers would not work any longer, and now this ten-year-old wanted a full explanation of her mother's early life. Like all innocents, she, too, thought there must be a logical explanation for the unimaginable. Who knows, maybe she secretly hoped that if there was no evidence, she wouldn't think her mother was guilty.

"I wish you were from somewhere else." That was understandable.

But you can't choose the place you were born. It's just there. It was a village alongside a river that for thousands of years had carved its way through the sandy soil, repeatedly claiming more land, replacing dunes with floodplains. Atop one of the remaining sandy hills sat the village. Where the river came closest, often threatening the lower-lying areas, an embankment had been built to hold back the destructive force of the current. The retaining wall bordered the main street and provided the inhabitants of the lower village with convenient outdoor seating. Day in and day out, the old folks in the village occupied their usual places, chewing over tidbits of news and gossip and offering these up in the hope that somebody would come and chat a while. The come-on usually started with: Have you heard…?

Or, when the funeral bell had sounded: Do you know who it's for?

The main street ran from the Village Hall up past the Protestant church to the cemetery that was on somewhat higher ground in order to protect the dead from groundwater that could rise three feet or more during floods.

Once, in the spring of '26, the water did reach the graves, and after it had receded, the gravediggers had to spend weeks reburying the bones that had gotten stuck in the boxwood hedges and potted plants. The flood stories—and they were numerous—became the main topic as soon as the wall-sitters spotted the first tree limbs floating by. "There goes the riverbank" they'd say, and people in the lower part of town would start clearing out their cellars.

That part of the village stretched out along the river, crisscrossed by a tangle of narrow alleyways that turned into such a maze that, after nightfall, only a local could find his way through the connecting passageways into the upper town. It was said that many a young man from one of the neighboring villages had made a wrong turn in the dark and never found his way out.

Such people were known as "imports." You could tell them from the natives because of the way they talked; for example, their inability to pronounce their "r's" correctly—a defect that forever branded them as foreigners.

Being a foreigner meant not having a past, never being mentioned by Margarethe Steiger, known to the locals as "Tall Gret," who knew the town's public records by heart and who had the details of every local story stashed in her long-term memory. "That's the way it was, I'm telling you," she always said—thus dismissing any other version. It can't be proved that it had rained cats and dogs—as if God Almighty had opened all the spigots!—when her youngest niece was born. But there is evidence that the child had resisted entry into the world, still visible in the hairline scar over her left eyebrow, a blemish the midwife always stared at when they unavoidably met on the street, as if the child had deliberately ruined her handiwork.

Oma Stina, who had birthed her youngest all by herself in a potato field, would have handled things differently if she had gotten there earlier. But since she had to come from some distance away (her daughter, the child's mother, was a village "import"), and had to make a detour at the mill and then double back across a field because the street was under water, her advice to the midwife about the delivery came too late. She did not, however, arrive too late to represent the maternal side of the family with regard to naming rights.

The midwife, who usually tried to avoid interfering in family matters, later reported that, in this case, she had no choice but to intervene energetically, since Oma Stina was livid and hollering at the young mother lying there ill with childbed fever.

Marga? What a ridiculous name, she thundered. Whose crazy idea was that? Tall Gret had gotten there first, and since in the village everyone's name got shortened no matter what, she had generously offered to bestow the first two syllables of her own name upon the child. And why not? She was, after all, the eldest sister of the child's father, whose mother had died giving birth to him.

As befitting such a scene, there were some heavy sighs, and the wine bottle that always stood ready for anyone thirsty was passed around. Questioning glances were exchanged, and everyone decided to move on.

But, of course, Oma Stina couldn't let it go at that. She marched down into the lower town to have a talk with Greta. Naturally, she couldn't just barge in and come out with it, so she first inquired about how things were going. Just to be polite, she also accepted a glass of Gimmeldinger Meerspinne. And so it happened that, in the course of the conversation about the terrible potato harvest, and about the cross that everyone must bear (Stina's cross being an unmarried daughter and a son who liked to have a few drinks too many), the time passed, during which the groundwater continued to rise, flooding Greta's root cellar, threatening her meager store of potatoes and vegetables for the winter. Oma Stina then helped rescue what could be salvaged. It was not much.

Only later did Tante Greta learn that that very afternoon the baby had been registered at the town hall as Christina Margarethe. Oma Stina had given the child her own full, unabbreviated name. That's the way it was, I'm telling you. And if there hadn't been a flood, Greta's niece would have had a different name.

What this Tante Greta would never admit is that she could barely contain her schadenfreude when she heard that the child's father had refused to have her baptized. After all, it is only through the rite of baptism that one is officially authorized to meddle fully in the life of a newly anointed child.

Oma Stina would never be able to forgive her son-in-law, and time and again she would remind him that the Good Lord above— punctuating this reference with her index finger pointed heavenward—would take pity on the poor heathen child and that she, Stina, would do her best to remind Him of that every Sunday.

But when her fervent Sunday prayers failed to have any visible effect on her granddaughter's cradle cap, she had an ointment made by Susie, the herbalist, and diligently rubbed this on the baby's scalp every day, declaring that God sometimes needed earthly assistance.

A child's most laudable attribute is its ability to adapt itself to its surroundings. This was called being "well-behaved." And Christina was well-behaved, except that she constantly pulled and tugged at her crocheted and knitted caps, signaling that she preferred to go bareheaded—which, of course, was not allowed. The cradle cap had advanced to hair-loss, and no family likes to show off a bald-headed baby.

When her hair finally grew back in, it was ash-blonde and not at all like the hair she had lost, a rich chestnut brown like that of her parents. Even Susie the herbalist had to admit that in all the years she had been practicing, never had she seen anything like it.

This was one of the changes that the child didn't notice, along with the loss of bone density that gave her spine a slight curvature. As treatment for this, Doctor Müller prescribed a sunlamp, milk from Oma Stina's goats, and rest.

What the child needed was rest! So the window shutters were drawn, the doorbell disconnected, and everyone tiptoed around so as

not to disturb the child. No wonder, then, that the child had little interest in going to sleep in the evening and would instead lean over
the side of her crib so she could watch the moving shadows through
the frosted glass panes in the door. It would not be long before such
maneuvers would lead to her falling headfirst out of bed. She was
not only told of this having happened, but also remembered it. It must
have left an indelible impression, since Christina always attributed
her lifelong fear of heights to this fall into the abyss.

But she didn't remember—or rather, suppressed—the fact that
from then on she was tightly strapped into her crib.

The girl really is absentminded, no two ways about it. She'd forget
her own head if it weren't attached to her shoulders! How often had
she been reminded that the way home from kindergarten was straight
down Alte Schulstrasse, a route that even a dawdling four-year-old
should be able to cover in ten minutes.

Where can she be?

She's in the castle garden, which unauthorized persons are not
permitted to enter. But since she can't yet read, the world is still open
to her. She even walks on the grass and picks a few daisies. The castle, inherited by the von Gondelheims, now houses the District Home
for the Blind. Once a year, the village housewives are invited to come
in—through the entrance to the horse stalls—to buy straw brooms
and woven baskets made by the residents. These residents can't read
the warning notices either, but they have been trained to walk hand
in hand, sticking to the gravel paths and keeping each other from
breaking any of the rules. Christina's mother, who in the meantime
has searched up and down Alte Schulstrasse, must once again suffer
being lectured by Herr Heidlauf, Superintendent for the Blind, that

she must make it clear to the child, sooner rather than later, that she is now, and always will be, a trespasser.

I will, Herr Heidlauf, I'll do my best.

And now, Christina wants to find her way home with her eyes closed. Lately, she has been depending more on her nose than her eyes. She won't eat a thing without first sniffing it.

The soup smells burned!

No, it just scorched a bit on the bottom of the pot. She should count herself lucky to have something to eat!

And now, here we go again, an invocation of the bad old days. Back then, oh, back then. A sigh, then another, and another, because back then there was nothing to eat but potatoes and salt, sometimes not even that.

Why can't parents ever figure out that such stories—tales of going hungry way back when, or in some other country—will never convince a child to eat her spinach rather than play with it, her fork making a lovely crosshatch pattern? Christina chokes on every bite. Her mother then starts in on her litany of if-then sentences, such as: If you don't eat, then you'll starve, then you'll be like Skinny-Kaspar.

Christina was one of the countless German children who had gotten the *Struwelpeter* book for Christmas. In it, Kaspar (the first documented case of anorexia) ends up dying because he refuses to eat his soup. There's also little Pauline who, despite the warnings of her parents and her cats, Minz and Maus, plays with matches and ends up reduced to a pile of ashes.

Christina will bequeath her unabridged, full-color edition of *The Whimsical and Merry Tales of Struwelpeter* to her cousin Erika, who always eats her soup and who, at the dinner table, only speaks when spoken to—and then only haltingly. The fact that Erika later ended up being held back in first grade was balm to Christina's soul. Less out of schadenfreude than because this development contradicted her mother's dictum that well-behaved children are rewarded. Being held back is hardly a reward. Rewards come in many forms, but only to children who have learned how to avoid falling into puddles in this village without a proper drainage system.

In this town, no transgression remained private—everybody knew everything. Elise, your young one has fallen into a puddle again and is screaming her head off because she's afraid to come home.

Some news was broadcast from windowsill to windowsill every morning when it was time to air out the bedding. Official news was announced by Seppel, the town clerk. Gossip was exchanged sotto voce over the garden fence or in doorways. Information from the outside world was relayed by Gretel, the postmistress, who, owing to her official duties, had a jump on everybody.

Even Elise, who repeatedly claimed she wanted nothing to do with village gossip—an "import" like her had to exercise restraint in such things!—gave in every so often and lingered at the window of Frau Althaus, the village seamstress. Despite Frau Althaus's harelip and the row of stickpins that she clasped between her misshapen lips, Elise managed to hear about the recent brawl between the Reds and the Brownshirts. While her mother was listening, Christina took the opportunity to slip out of her hand and once again promptly fell into a puddle.

Christina can still dimly remember the puddle episodes, but nothing about the bar brawls in the Gasthaus zum Pflug. Nor does she have any memory of the Communist Party demonstration in the civic stadium, where Ernst Thälmann[1] supposedly held her aloft in his arms. Only later would she learn that she was a Communist child. A Communist child has a father who often goes to meetings and a mother who carries banners at rallies while worrying that things will

---

[1] The Communists' candidate in the two 1932 presidential elections that pitted Hitler (only recently become a German citizen) against Hindenburg, the candidate of both Social Democrats and the Catholic Center. (Fritz Stern, *Five Germanies I Have Known* [New York: Farrar, Straus and Giroux, 2006] 84).

turn out badly. The toy chest of a Communist child will prove to be a perfect hiding place for leaflets as well as for party badges with which she can adorn her doll's dresses.

This doll, another Christmas present, was named Bärbel. She was made of celluloid and had eyes of blue glass and two very red lips. To judge from all the grown-ups' self-satisfied clucking, it was clear to Christina that this doll was meant to fulfill her every wish.

Not really. Christina had actually wanted an erector set. Instead she got this Bärbel, who was supposed to bring out her maternal instincts. The grown-ups also provided stage directions: Dress her up! Undress her! Rock her to sleep! Sing her a lullaby! And then, when her birthday present was a rattan doll carriage: Take her out for a walk! Show her off!

This script, passed down for generations, complete with all the visual and aural cues, was one that all the women in the family had learned by heart. No deviations were allowed. Certainly not, for instance, dismemberment, which Christina periodically undertook and which often sent Bärbel to the doll hospital.

She was playing with Bärbel when the men in jackboots raided the apartment, rummaged through the desk, and searched the bookcase without noticing the child and her doll, who watched them through the doorway. Her mother, wringing her hands, paced up and down the hall until she noticed that one of the SA men was about to yank from the wardrobe a packet of freshly laundered bed linens that she had tied together with ribbon. That was the last straw.

Grabbing him from behind by his shoulder-strap, she dragged the intruder away from the wardrobe through the bedroom door into the hall. He found himself on the losing end of the ensuing melee and crashed to the floor next to the clothes tree, under which the cowering child sat with her fingers stuck in her ears. She could only look on as the doll's face was smashed flat under the man's weight.

Christina is reported to have screamed so loudly that all the neighbors came running, whereupon the SA men nonchalantly took off, as if they could have cared less. She was promised a new doll, but she refused. Instead, she would finally get her erector set.

But first her father's room had to be put back in order. Her mother's obsession with tidiness was usually severely constrained in there, because her father did not want a neatly ordered room and had made that perfectly clear to his Elise umpteen times. But today she threw caution to the wind and got to work. This time, there would be no argument, because Christina's father didn't come home.

He was in protective custody, though it was not at all clear to Christina whom her father needed protection from. He was being held in the county jail, and her mother was supposed to bring him his toiletries and cigarettes. Christina was allowed to go along.

She had brought a sweet roll along in her pocket for him. But children weren't allowed inside the "County," so they let her sit out in the waiting room where she ate the sweet roll herself. She chewed very slowly so that it would last a long time. She was a child who could wait patiently, and for that, she was rewarded. On the way home, for the very first time, she was allowed to ask for her own ticket from the streetcar conductor.

Elise could report to the family members, who were gathered in the kitchen to help see her through this difficult time, that Christina was getting more sensible every day.

For heaven's sake, Philipp should just keep his mouth shut; after all, he's a businessman, and besides, he should think about his responsibilities to his family. You just can't swim against the current; and besides, what good is it going to do? It's just asking for trouble.

Everyone assembled agreed that resistance was no longer possible and that they would simply have to go along in order to get along. They could still demonstrate their lack of enthusiasm by not hanging the flag out nor otherwise decorating the house for the parade that had been announced for the following Saturday.

Later on, one would in fact see a few little Nazi flags fluttering in Onkel Adam's window boxes. Not that that would surprise Philipp, who as early as 1932, in a heated conversation with his brother, had labeled the Social Democrats, the Communists' rivals, as "Social Fascists."

But things had not yet gotten that bad. For now, the geraniums in Onkel Adam's window boxes were blooming without the protection of little Nazi flags. For now, as they sit in the visiting room at the county jail, Philipp feels free to share with his wife his reaction to the family's political equivocation: The whole lot of them can all go to hell! Whether or not Christina got the real drift of these conversations back and forth around the kitchen table is unknown.

What we do know: she stopped asking when her father would be coming back. Instead, in kindergarten, she started building trains, ones so long that Sister Bertha had to reprimand her for taking all the building blocks away from the other children.

Sister Bertha, trained in the ways of the soul, taught Christina to pray. Fervently, as she demonstrated, with eyes closed: *Now I lay me down to sleep, I pray the Lord my soul to keep.*

The Lord was also keeping watch in Tante Greta's room, hanging on the wall over the double bed. Dressed in a blue cloak, crook in hand, He was shepherding a flock of children over a field dotted with sheep. Christina wanted to believe He was in heaven. She also wanted to know how He could stay up there without falling from the sky. She quickly figured that out on the day the first Zeppelin hovered over the village.

He's sitting in there! This she supposedly told the kindergarten teacher, who, despite her best efforts, had trouble imagining the Lord as commander of the Reich's first fleet of dirigibles. Tante Lisa, however, found it hilarious and added this pearl of juvenile wisdom to her little blue notebook, where it joined the strand of pearls that—as she boasted to her sister Elise—her son, Ernst August, regularly came up with. Ach! Love is blind! Tante Lisa was walking proof of that as far as Elise was concerned. But how can you tell your own sister that her son seemed not quite right in the head ever since his bout of meningitis? You also cannot tell her that for these last few months you haven't been able to laugh at anything. All you can do is sit at the kitchen table and cry.

Children get upset when mothers cry. They can't help but feel that they're somehow responsible for those tears. But not for long, since Tante Lisa chooses this moment to give Christina the giant sack of candy all German children get when they start elementary school. Tomorrow is the first day, and she can eat the whole thing then! But only after the school photographer has taken a picture of her in her new smocked dress, white cabled knee socks, and black patent-leather shoes. Okay? Okay!

The poor thing, sighs Lisa to her sister as she fits a Camel into the gold cigarette holder that she ever so graciously holds between her thumb and her lapis lazuli-ringed middle finger. She'll give the lapis lazuli ring to Christina someday, if she's a good girl and stops playing with the neighborhood hooligans. It's high time, Lisa suggests, that the girl start acting her age and stop running around like a little gooseherd.

The reference to geese was intentional, since every morning Christina would lead Tante Eva's geese down to the river. But she soon stopped doing that. Not because of Tante Lisa's criticism, but because Hans, the gander, had started chasing her.

Tante Lisa blathers on and on. As soon as Philipp comes back—and that must be soon because Attorney Bauer must have filed an appeal by now—Elise must put her foot down; things simply cannot go on this way. He gets himself into trouble with all his political nonsense. It will be the death of him!

Elise once more quietly wipes her right eye with the corner of her apron and with her left glances over to the chaise where her daughter sits biting her fingernails.

Lisa, the child!

They tell her to go out into the hallway and check in Tante Lisa's handbag to see what she's brought for her. Christina finds an Eduscho picturebook that shows little Negroes picking coffee beans. Eduscho is the coffee with the best aroma! That much she knows. What she'd like to know is what they're whispering about in the kitchen. This top-secret conversation ends abruptly when the Eduscho picturebook comes flying across the table, narrowly missing Tante Lisa's head before knocking over the vase of catkins standing on the kitchen counter.

Is that what you call gratitude? More an accusation than a question. Did you ever see such a thing? The little monster attacking her own aunt! What else will we have to put up with? Just wait till your father hears about this!

Go on! Go on and tell him! Write to him in Kislau![2]

Now where had the girl heard that?

---

[2] *Kislau* was a regional workhouse/concentration camp located in Kislau Castle, originally a hunting lodge in the state of Württemberg and about twenty-five miles from Christina's home. From 1933-39, it primarily housed German political opponents of the Nazi regime. When the camp closed in 1939, its remaining prisoners were transferred to the Dachau concentration camp. The narrative suggests that Christina was not aware of what "Kislau" meant but rather had just heard the name and made assumptions about what her father might/must be doing there. (https://www.frankfallaarchive.org/prisons/kislau-workhouse/)

My father is in Kislau, she explained to Herr Schroth, the baker, when she went to get bread the next morning. We're going to visit him. A father has not really disappeared as long as he can be reached by train. My father is building a house there, she told the baker.

Now she's done it. Once again her willful nature allowed her to manipulate reality so that she could deny what was upsetting her.

Baker Schroth, looking as always like he had just escaped from a sack of flour, leaned over the counter and offered her a chocolate cookie with his chalk-white hand. This is for you, little one.

No information is ever really lost from one's memory. What is lost is the ability to retrieve it. She could remember nothing about this visit to Kislau. Every effort to unearth the details was unsuccessful. You were there, insists Christina's mother, whose own recall of this particular occasion was complete in every detail.

It was after Hitler's power grab, shortly before the Reichstag elections in 1933. She had used a copy of *The Worker's News*—the headline: "A Vote for Hitler is a Vote for War!"—to wrap one of Oma Stina's homemade liver sausages to take to her husband. On that same day, there was a silent demonstration in Kislau in response to the murder of a comrade. As a result, the prison commandant had ordered a week of confinement, with no written communication and no visitors allowed. Mother and daughter, therefore, had had to return home having accomplished nothing.

Because Christina had cried the whole way back, next time she would be left behind with Tante Eva where she could play in the yard after school. With the ants, that is. And not exactly playing. She had blocked their path so that the column had to find an alternate route around the barricade. A scouting party was sent ahead to figure out the lay of the land, while the rest of the ant colony scurried around, desperate for a leader they could follow.

That's just plain torture, shouted Tante Eva from the chicken yard, where she was introducing her newest chicks to the other chickens. In a wire cage, of course, so that the older ones couldn't harm the youngsters.

Tante Eva knew about those in need of protection. She had taken in two young children whose mother, a distant cousin of her husband, had left them sitting on the dock in Bremen when she sailed off to America with a lover. Such is life, child, Tante Eva would say, such is life. But then: "Never you mind, vengeance is for the Lord," her usual response to deal with any situation that called for retribution.

Tante Eva had raised Christina's father after their mother died giving birth to this last, change-of-life baby. She took in other people's children, while all she could do for her own was plant for-get-me-nots on their graves. Liesl, her first-born, had died of pneu-monia. How often had Tante Eva taken the picture of Liesl lying in her casket out of the ornately decorated cigar box to fondle it in her rough, scarred hands as she wept? It was testimony that, before Christina, there had been another child who brought her nettles from the riverbank to help fatten up the chicks and turn them into laying hens. Had Liesl also tortured the ants? Of course not. Like all the dead, she was faultless. Her grave lay just to the right of the cemetery entrance, three rows in front of Hans, the son and heir, who had died of typhoid. What Tante Eva would not, or could not, ever admit was that she had given him poppyseed tea in a little bag to suck on, so that he'd take long afternoon naps while she worked in the cigar fac-tory to earn a little money on the side.

This way of getting children to nap resulted in the death of a number of village children, until a woman from the welfare office went house to house cautioning mothers.

Christina knew nothing of the pain suffered by her favorite aunt, the surrogate mother who tenderly brushed Christina's blonde hair from her face and let her hold a little chick, promising her that it was her very own. The fact that Christina was always so attached to Tante Eva was something Elise could never quite get over.

It's too bad that chicks grow up to be chickens who eat the newly sprouted lettuce and soil the clean wash laid out on the grass to bleach. One chicken's time has come, and neither pleas nor tears do any good.

At Sunday dinner, to which Tante Lisa and her family are invited, Christina sits, red-eyed from crying, and decorates the rim of her plate with bits and pieces of her vegetable soup. Eat, so you'll be big and strong, admonishes her mother.

But how can you swallow anything when chicken fricassee is being served, and you're the only mourner at this Sunday's feast? Christina is sent to her room, where she rips all the pages off the calendar, as if that would eliminate all the coming Sundays. Christina is hard-headed. She's obstinate, furious. Once again, her mother wields her arsenal of adjectives. It's high time you come to your senses. Once school starts, they'll knock these silly ideas out of you.

From a third grader, she learns that Herr Glaser has a stick he uses to rap you on your knuckles. He even slaps you, says Kurt Keil during a game of marbles. Kurt knows about that firsthand, since he doesn't have a father who would make it his business to confront Herr Glaser on his way home and threaten to punish him if he should ever have the audacity to lay a hand on his child.

Punishment is something that fathers are responsible for. Mothers hold back, or suggest mitigating circumstances, even though they started the whole thing.

Is it absolutely necessary to tell Father that Christina, his dearest daughter (emphasis on *dearest*), has stolen five pennies from his skat winnings for reasons she has yet to explain? Caught red-handed and showing no remorse, she takes off without saying a word. Were there other words to be said? Of course there were.

Just wait till your father comes home. Then things will get back to normal.

Christina came to recognize the conflicted feeling of hoping that life would again return to normal without knowing exactly what the adults meant by "normal."

Still worried, Christina waited near Herr Jakoby's barnyard gate for him to return from the fields with his horses. As soon as she spotted the farmer driving his team of white horses, she flicked her thumb with the tip of her tongue, then began pounding her open left hand with her right fist, reciting the familiar good-luck chant: *White horse, white horse, bad luck flee, bring good fortune home to me!*

It will never be known whether it was by chance or through divine intervention, but one afternoon her father appeared in their yard. No matter how he got there, the main thing was that he was home and could admire the asparagus bed that Elise had planted in the sandy corner of the yard next to the raspberry bushes. The asparagus aren't ready yet, but I will make you creamed spinach with roast potatoes, she promises her husband—a scaffold of skin and bones sitting there on the garden bench.

The daughter, meanwhile, observes the scene through the tomato plants, then strategically withdraws into the row of pole beans. She busies herself pulling weeds, something she would never do under ordinary circumstances, despite her mother's constant nagging. She would leave it to the grown-ups to get everything back to normal.

Only when it's getting dark does she venture back into the house, where once again cigarette smoke hangs in the air, and where her father sits at the kitchen table slurping his oatmeal, and where, for once, her mother lets the sound of his slurping go by without making a comment. Nothing is said, either, about the fact that her father sits quietly for weeks on end, playing chess against himself with the pieces he had whittled in solitary confinement, seemingly unable to find his way back into the daily routine.

It was mid-summer before Christina could again take his thermos of tea to the building site. She was again allowed to help stir the concrete and to climb around the new building. But the foreman, Herr Feuerstein, warned her not to touch the plumb line. He was responsible for getting the walls straight and demonstrated his eagle eye by regularly spitting within a hair's breadth of Christina's head. The foreman had little tolerance for children. Even less for Jews. He could do without the whole lot of them. This opinion was intended for his boss, Philipp, who had recently started storing his building materials in widow Kahn's shed and where the foreman now had to go to pick up the framing boards.

The widow Kahn lived on Judenstrasse in one of those little slanting houses, each seeming to hold up the neighboring one, since none of them could depend on their foundations, eroded by countless floodings.

If it weren't for the synagogue, her architect father said, the whole mess would have collapsed by now.

The villagers had nothing to do with the inhabitants of these houses. All Christina knew was that they were all elderly, shriveled-up little people who sometimes were spotted trudging along the main street on their way to the Jewish cemetery, which was on the other side of the river.

Tante Eva said that old Herr Kahn, who had formerly owned the cigar factory, had recently passed away and that Onkel Karl had laid a wreath on his grave, a wreath from the volunteer fire department, where Herr Kahn had been an honorary member. He is better off now, her aunt declared, recalling her former employer. As they say, the old folks die off and the young ones take off. Frau Rosenmeyer, who sold the notions that the villagers depended on (imagine the whole town without shoelaces, without elastic garters or suspenders!), and who provided the easy credit that allowed almost everyone to buy on account, had also suddenly disappeared under cover of night, even though she was married to a gentile.

Christina wants to know from Tante Eva whether Herr and Frau Rosenmeyer being married amounts to "shaming the race"—a concept proclaimed by her teacher, Herr Bohrer, that needed examples. Christina knew the word "shame"—children were often warned about bringing shame to the family—but what did "shame" have to do with "race"? Regardless, Christina wants to be Aryan, since that means pure—almost like being nobility, was how her teacher had described it. During recess, a hastily appointed committee examines her and finds her to be without blemish, except for a few little moles, but they were just inherited and didn't really count—Onkel Adam, in fact, has twenty-three of them on his back in the shape of the Ursa Major constellation.

Tante Eva says she has no idea what "shaming the race" might mean, so when Christina gets home, she tries to look into her own family tree. She is particularly interested in a distant cousin of her mother who had married a wealthy man from Frankfurt. What was his name again? Gleisberg, right? Is that an Aryan name? But instead of being reassured that no one in her family had brought shame to the race, she is told that in this house they never want to hear those words mentioned again. There are a lot of things that are not supposed to be mentioned. Christina decides to categorize her experiences with such things. For example, there are topics discussed at home that are preceded by "Now, don't you dare repeat this." For example, "There's bound to be a war." This would have been a nice little tidbit to trot out at school, but her father's warning keeps her from saying anything. Thus, she becomes more and more reticent in class, a fact noted by her teacher, who, while duly promoting Christina into the third grade, writes on her report card that this pupil's diligence and enthusiasm seem to have waned.

You can say that again, her mother thought, since lately little Miss Fancy Pants also seems to have waning interest in doing her chores around the house. If you send her to water the garden in the vacant lot they had recently bought next to the cemetery, you'll find that she has left the hose running in the furrow and has wandered off somewhere. If Frau Ries hadn't happened by and turned off the water, the lettuce sprouts would have drowned.

Where has she wandered off to? Just over to the canal bridge, where the village kids meet up every afternoon to find out which of the gang has enough nerve to jump off the upper part of the bridge. Of course, in order to do that, you have to climb up steel rafters that are hot as coals on the soles of your feet. Then the plunge into the abyss, arms pressed to your sides, down to the slimy canal bottom, then popping up to the surface to be rewarded by the cheers of the onlookers.

If their mothers had known what was meant by "test of courage," if they had had any idea of the dangers their children were exposing themselves to just to show that they weren't cowards, what would those mothers have done? Probably nothing. Maybe given the older ones a good talking-to, and the younger ones a good spanking?

"Weakness must be driven out. The youth of Germany should be subjected to the most severe tests in order to overcome the fear of death." Waldemar Vondung, just recently promoted to leader in the German Youngsters,[3] is quoting the Führer. Fear of death: this is

---

[3] The *Deutsches Jungvolk in der Hitler Jugend* ("German Youngsters in the Hitler Youth") [also DJ or DJV] was the separate section for boys aged ten to fourteen of the Hitler Youth organization in Nazi Germany. Through a program of outdoor activities, parades, and sports, it aimed to indoctrinate its young members in

Fatherland

something Christina wrestles with nightly when she has bad dreams. Being scared of dying, is there anything worse? Yes, there is. Waldemar's contemptuous look when it's her turn again and she gets scared halfway up and slides back down. When he looks away in disgust, her fear of being an outcast overcomes her fear of the jump. She tries it again and does it!

It seems that a mother doesn't want to know everything that is happening in her daughter's life, although in this case Elise must have noticed that after that particular afternoon, Christina was walking tall. Christina even ignored the fuss about the half-drowned lettuce without her usual attempt to justify the error of her ways.

Christina basked in the glow of what had taken place: Waldemar's approving hand on her shoulder signaled her ascent into a higher realm. Only those who were able to jump off the bridge could avoid the dangerous propellers of the tugboats to swim up alongside the barges, letting the wake thrust them up onto the sidewalls of the lock. There they would lie, exhausted, until the lock-keeper's bell signaled them to jump off.

The canal now belonged to the brave ones. It had been built after the last major flood to divert the course of the river whose "idyllic caressing curve" (as described in the local history guide) at flood stage slowly strangled the village. The village was now an island, and the young islanders guarded its waterways. They knew the boatmen by name, and pity whoever was naïve enough to think they could keep the kids off the lock by smearing tar on the sides. The boatmen could be dead sure the next time they navigated the lock that their wheelhouse would be pelted with stones, or they'd find the lock's entrance dammed up with reed rafts that the youthful militia had assembled at the river's edge.

the tenets of Nazi ideology. Membership became fully compulsory for eligible boys in 1939. By the end of World War II, some had become child soldiers. (https://en.wikipedia.org/wiki/Deutsches_Jungvolk)

21

The boatmen gained nothing by swearing and ultimately suc-cumbed to the superior forces.

It was clear to Christina that her parents actually had two daughters: one who was strong and courageous, second in command of the reed-raft fleet; the other, dumb as they come. It was this "dummy"—the word had once again slipped out of her mother's mouth—whose dropped stitches in the potholders she was making had to be picked up by her mother—even though Christina was sure to drop them once again.

It was these potholders with their perforated pattern that Tante Greta got for her fiftieth birthday and which she found quite original. Tante Anna commented that Christina had obviously not inherited her mother's domestic skills, a remark that caused Elise to hold her breath to keep from bursting out laughing. But the laughing stopped as soon as Christina started to recite the poem she had written for Tante Greta:

> *Fifty years you're old today,*
> *Many hard times along the way,*
> *Sometimes you're warm and sometimes cold,*
> *What mood awaits we're never told,*
> *But still and all we love you lots,*
> *Dear Tante Greta, you are tops.*

The silence is deafening until Tante Greta gets the festivities going again with her observation that the rhyming was excellent. With that unerring ability that children have to sense the mood of adults, Christina realizes that her performance in her aunt's garden had not made her very popular. What she doesn't understand is the reason for Tante Greta's increasingly bad mood.

Onkel Karl, it seems, has cheated on her with Katie Gutmann, the woman who has been keeping the village supplied with notions ever since Frau Rosenmeyer disappeared. Tante Greta had immediately smelled a rat when she came home after work at the cigar factory and found Katie in her kitchen showing Karl the latest fashion in suspenders. There he stood in his underwear while Katie supposedly took his measurements. Greta had thrown the adulteress out of the house along with her case of samples. For days, the neighbors could find thread, razor blades, and other odds and ends scattered in the street. Greta told them to keep everything they found—her husband had already paid for it. That's how it was!

Onkel Karl has come home from work earlier than usual for the birthday party and meekly presents his wife with a bouquet of pink hydrangeas, whereupon she haughtily directs him to the children's table where he has to sit on a little stool, rather lost in his own thoughts, wolfing down three pieces of Frankfurter kringle. Christina herself is on an eating spree for a change. But Tante Anna eats the most. She needs to tank up, so to speak, since lately she has been saving every penny, skimping on food in order to finance the addition to her house. She is building up and out—three stories—so she can take in renters to help pay off the mortgage more quickly. Tante Anna gets away with doing what Christina is not allowed to do, namely, talk with her mouth full. Besides, Tante Anna is stingy. Even on festival days when one is expected to give something to the children, she won't give them so much as a penny. She won't come to the door when you ring the bell—it's always then that she claims to have a migraine. But it's not because of migraines that she's not eating, Tante Eva had learned. She just can't afford it, the poor thing.

So, Christina lets Tante Anna have a seventh piece of cake and awards her first place on her list of gluttons.

Thin as a rail, Tante Anna is invited to the next Shrove Tuesday buffet where she surveys the various courses, hiding a toothless smile behind her hand, because she only puts in her dentures when it's time to eat.

Congratulations to Tante Anna. She'll make it through the coming lean years with flying colors, since she has already learned during the good years how to go hungry.

The rest of the Germans weren't going hungry any longer, and the fourth grade knew who was responsible for that. The Führer, of course! His picture hung over the blackboard, his head crowned with a golden laurel wreath, his eyes cast toward the windows. He appeared to gaze into the future, a future that Fräulein Barth promised would be glorious. The fourth graders knew, of course, what the term "glorious" meant, as well as its opposites, such as "dishonorable," "infamous," "shameful"—terms that described the recent past and which their teacher carefully wrote out in old-fashioned German cursive on the blackboard.

Fräulein Barth, like most of the teachers in the village, was an import. She lived in a little alley near the Catholic church in a one-story house whose roof had been built out with dormers to create a single attic room. It's here that she gives voice lessons on Tuesdays and Thursdays, but only to those who either have musical talent or who are the daughters of Nazi Party comrades, like Annemarie Engel, who always sings off-key but claims she's singing harmony.

On Saturdays, Fräulein Barth sits up there and makes note of the names of pupils who go to confession. For her, there is only one sin, and that is failing to assume the correct posture when pledging allegiance to the flag.

Surely one could expect German children to stand at attention for a few minutes, particularly on the Führer's birthday. Yes, one could, if only the back row would stop fooling around. If looks could kill, the entire fourth grade would have died on the spot. Rector Herrmann, the acting local group leader, must have consulted with Fräulein Barth, because in his remarks, he, too, emphasizes the glorious future. Annemarie Engel, the mayor's daughter, is allowed to approach the flag. The uniformed older pupils march in an open square around the flagpole. Hail to the flag!

The school choir chimes in under the direction of Fräulein Barth, whose extraordinarily large bosom seems to stretch from sea to shining sea.[4] The buttonholes on her fine silk blouse strain with each beat as she conducts, so that by the time the choir gets to the line "Deutschland, Deutschland über alles," the little mother-of-pearl buttons have reached their limit, and Fräulein Barth is left standing before the assembled group with her brassiere showing.

Under the circumstances, they skip the *Horst-Wessel-Lied*.[5]

News of the incident swept through the village like wildfire. After that, Fräulein Barth didn't dare appear in public, much less in the school, and was soon transferred to Hamburg.

That was a crying shame, because the substitute sent by the district school administration was a certain Herr Petersen, an ethnic German who had returned to the Reich for the express purpose of tormenting its youth—at least that's what the fourth graders thought.

Homework must be turned in before class, written out perfectly in ink. Ink splotches lower your grade. Giggling is not allowed. Needs of a personal nature have to be postponed until the break. Herr Petersen has no sympathy for weak bladders. Christina gives Hilde Schwarz a telling look, since up until now she has always been allowed to slip out of the classroom without asking for permission. She suffers from some condition. But despite this, Hilde is really pretty. Just like her mother, Mrs. Schwarz the beautician, who takes good care of herself, always looks the picture of health,

---

[4] In the German text, the description of the extent of Fräulein Barth's bosom playfully includes the well-known line from the 1841 *Deutschlandlied* by August Heinrich Hoffmann von Fallersleben: "von der Maas bis an die Memel."

[5] The anthem of the Nazi Party; from 1933-45, also the co-national anthem of Germany, along with the first stanza of the *Deutschlandlied*. (https://en.wikipedia.org/wiki/Horst-Wessel-Lied)

and keeps trying to introduce the village women to the latest in skin and hair care.

She maintains that it is one's hair that lends the face its character. Ladies, you really should consider Seebald's hair coloring. I have it available in the salon for only three Reichsmarks.

Mrs. Schwarz uses it herself, as Christina learns from Hilde, who gives Christina countless sample bottles of haircare preparations, always assuring her that her mother's magnificent head of hair is the result of a product patented by the German Reich. In return for the samples, Christina has to watch out for Hilde and press a ruler on her tongue whenever she has a seizure and falls off the school bench, white as a ghost. There is nothing to be done except wait until Hilde opens her eyes again. Christina makes that quite evident to Herr Petersen, who has rather awkwardly tried to help Christina grab Hilde under her arms as if she were a marionette and place her back on the bench.

Children who have a problem during class may now once again go do what they need to do, and whenever Hilde gets up to meekly ask permission to leave, the teacher immediately lets Christina go out with her. He must have noticed that Hilde always has to be excused whenever the class is doing arithmetic, something that of late is difficult for Christina Steiger, not to mention Hilde Schwarz. What he doesn't know is that at home Christina does her math assignments with a slide rule and, consequently, is having a terrible time with the long division exercises he assigned. But you need to be able to do long division if you want to go on to Gymnasium.[6]

---

[6] The German "classical" high school, with a focus on Greek and Latin, as well as mathematics and the natural sciences. Gymnasium studies began with the fifth year of school and lasted eight years, until grade thirteen. Successful Gymnasium graduates were awarded a diploma called the "Abitur," required for admission to university-level studies. In Germany at this time (and for many years after the war), admission to the Gymnasium was highly competitive, and those who did attend were overwhelmingly male and from the higher socio-economic classes.

The whole class could now figure out why Fräulein Steiger didn't have to bring a note when she was absent week before last. She would have preferred to keep it a secret in order to spare herself embarrassment if she failed the entrance exam. Annemarie Engel had experienced that in the extreme, and Christina was among those who had rather enjoyed Annemarie's misfortune.

Even now, at recess, Annemarie usually stands apart from her classmates, her arms stretched out along the wrought iron fence behind her. Such a sight ought to cause a girl to have a guilty conscience and feel sorry for the outcast, were it not for the other girls, who have nothing to regret and who link arms and draw Christina into their group.

That wasn't right. But what could she do?

Beyond the outskirts of the village, there was the city, for many centuries itself no more than a village of farmers and fishermen. But it had found favor with wealthy princes with impressive sounding names, and over time, by virtue of their privileged position, the town grew and annexed the neighboring villages. In the beginning, most of the villages vigorously resisted such attempts to incorporate them, but ultimately, they had to accede to the wishes of the city councillors. It was only the sorriest of these little villages—where every year on St. Martin's Day, Christina's ancestors had renewed their lease to operate the river ferry—that had remained independent, so that even today the inhabitants are proud to declare that they were never incorporated.

It's easy to understand, then, that the village inhabitants harbored a certain skepticism toward the city. You only went into the city when you had to, and you had to if you wanted a job. There were enormous factories there that every morning swallowed up the majority of the village's men, only to spit them back out in the evening. Then they'd bike home down Brückenstrasse, passing the war memorial before splitting up at Schlossstrasse. Some would stop in at their favorite tavern to have a drink.

One of these was Onkel Thomas, who had the reputation in the family of always being thirsty. Many an evening he would stumble along, pushing his bike past the cemetery where Christina and Tante Eva were watering the graves. Since Tante Greta's heart attack, Tante Eva had assumed the role of family matriarch, handling all the duties that went along with that job. One of those obligations was to take care of the family's cemetery plots. Judging from the inscriptions on the headstone, one of these plots was already rather overpopulated. It contained Christina's paternal grandparents, two of their infant children, and her grandfather's unmarried sister, who out of necessity had found her resting place there as well. In another spot lay Tante Eva's Hans and Liesl. Tante Eva had also taken on the care of neighboring graves because those weedy plots made the ones close by look bad. At least that's what Tante Eva thought. Promise me, Tina, that you'll take care of my grave when I'm gone. Plant a bleeding heart for me and put a simple wreath on my grave on All Saints' Day. Christina imagined a wreath made of evergreen boughs and dried elderberry blossoms mounted on a metal stand that would last all winter. She nodded in agreement and ran back to the spigot next to the mausoleum to fill up the watering can and drag it over to Hans' and Liesl's graves.

They gazed at her, their faces enameled onto little plaques atop their headstones, while Tante Eva, whose eyes had been treated with silver nitrate because of chronic eyelid infections, daubed her lashless eyelids with her apron sash and started in on the cemetery litany that Christina knew so well. It's true. We'll all die someday.

But where exactly is death lying in wait?

Readers of the *Munich Illustrated* know that last year there were 8,382 traffic deaths. They call that statistic a public health outrage.

People who step into the street from behind a parked car are putting themselves in danger. Hilde Seitz should have known that, in which case she would have crossed the street at the intersection, where the truck driver would have been able to see her and stop in time. There were no skid marks, just an outline of her crumpled body on the pavement. If only she had . . . . But she hadn't, and therefore she was now laid out in her parents' bedroom on a bed of white flowers with a bouquet of lilies-of-the-valley clasped in her wax-yellow hands. In order to make room, her parents' bed had been taken apart, stood up against the wall, and covered with white sheets. There were lit candles on the nightstands.

Lined up according to height at the head of her coffin were Hilde's siblings. Frau Seitz, her mother's cross pinned on the right lapel of her mourning dress, stroked her eldest's cheek and assured the mourners that her daughter had died instantly.

Christina wants to believe that. She also wants to leave but doesn't know exactly how to say goodbye. Under the circumstances, it hardly seems appropriate to say "Auf Wiedersehen, Hilde." With downcast eyes, she slowly inches her way backwards out of the room, then down the long, tiled hallway out into the courtyard.

Before crossing the street, she looks first to the left, then to the right. Clearly, she didn't really mean it when she told her parents the night before that she'd rather die than move into a house located next to a cemetery.

They told her she should at least look at the blueprints; the new house wouldn't have any windows overlooking the graves.

She didn't care. Being next to the cemetery was the same as being next to the dead, whether or not you could see the graves.

She could fuss all she wanted, but once they got the permit, the foundation would be poured. And that was final! There was no argument with her father's "final."

But then, when they got word from the Building Commission stating that an extension of Adolf-Hitler-Strasse was being planned, one that would cut off a substantial section of their lot, her father was convinced that, once again, he was being treated unfairly because of his political beliefs.

Christina, on the other hand, started to believe in guardian angels. Not the kind with little white wings sent by God. More like the birds that lived in the underbrush along the river's edge, where the great crested grebe nested and the Bohemian waxwing had left one of its yellow tail feathers in the flooded fishing boat, a feather that would be added to Christina's collection.

Christina also collected ideas, mostly from books, and used these to create for herself her own more perfect world. While reading Dumas' *Count of Monte Christo*, for example, she wallowed for days on end in an exaggerated sense of righteousness. Her response to any kind of request was "That's just not fair." For instance, she found it unfair that she should have to go and deliver the paychecks of her father's employees to their wives, just because the men would otherwise drink up the money in the Gasthaus zur Rose. The housing project where Herr Lohnert, the day-laborer, lived was located a little way outside the village and was reachable only by a well-trampled dirt path. In bad weather, shoes were likely to get muddy. In an effort to avoid the mud, Christina hopped from one grassy patch to another. In front of the brick building, children were playing in the puddles. They were barefoot, dirty—"neglected" was the term Christina thought of, but then dismissed, when she recognized one of her own outgrown dresses on one of the girls.

A snot-nosed boy stood in front of the worn wooden steps, his legs spread wide to block Christina's way. Who are you looking for?

The Lohnerts.

Down the hall, to the left.

The light was burned out in the hallway, and Christina had to feel her way along the wall to the door behind which Herr Lohnert lived with his family of seven. Frau Lohnert, answering Christina's knock and opening the door just a crack, wiped her hands on her apron and took the envelope in her hand with a firm nod of her head.

We do not know whether Frau Lohnert asked Christina to come in, or whether Christina was so overwhelmed by a desire to experience misery firsthand that she walked in uninvited. In any case, all of a sudden, there she was inside, and what she saw through the line of wash that hung across the room would become the standard against which she would measure every subsequent encounter with poverty. On the stove was a large washtub about to boil over, its lid rhythmically bobbing up and down. A little girl was lying on a narrow pallet next to the stove and seemed to be staring at the smoke that drifted from the cracked stovepipe toward the open window. The little girl tried to cough but was only able to produce a feeble wheeze that brought her head up from the pillow, only to let it fall back again. On the sooty wall to the right of the window hung a crucifix decorated with a palm frond, from which a steady stream of flies buzzed toward the infant who lay in a wash basket at the foot of the pallet. The baby batted at the insects with its little hands and feet, trying to defend itself. The air in the room took Christina's breath away. It was saturated by the sort of dampness that would cause things to breed and multiply—things that would stick to you if you couldn't escape.

It was just like in *Hanneles Himmelfahrt*,[7] she would later tell

---

[7] Popular play by Gerhart Hauptmann, premiered in 1893, with a child as the heroine.

her father as she tried to describe what she had seen. That was the first play he had taken her to the city to see. She had shed a few tears over Hannele, but this experience of harsh reality only filled her with a sense of fear and loathing.

It was probably around this same time that she agreed to accept the repeated overtures of friendship made by Trudy Wagner, whose twice-widowed mother barely managed to make ends meet by selling chicken feed. Christina helped Trudy drag the heavy sacks of feed to the washhouse. She also helped with the weighing and sometimes she waited on customers. She was even allowed to make change from the cigar box, since Trudy trusted Christina more than her own brother, who had sticky fingers and who no doubt would end up in jail.

Trudy not only had business smarts, she also knew an awful lot about things that adults talked about only among themselves, immediately changing the subject whenever a child came within earshot. Little bits of overheard conversations needed clarification, and Trudy has the knowledge that will help Christina fill in the blanks. Trudy can tell that Annemarie Fuchs is going to have a baby, even though she only wears loose-fitting smocks. Christina acts like she already knows that, but what she really wants to know is how you end up having a baby.

Unfortunately, Trudy was not really clear about that, but she did know how you didn't have a baby. For that, you went to the "angel-maker." Christina couldn't figure that out: How do you get to the end before the beginning? She had to try hard to block out the terrible thought that perhaps the little sister or brother she had for years been hoping for, and for whom she had been putting sugar cubes out on the windowsill, had become an angel. The whole idea that the stork plucked little children out of the big pond and set them down wherever he found sugar cubes . . . that didn't make any sense. No, Christina had never really believed that.

Sitting in Frau Wagner's sparkling clean kitchen, sharing their humble fare—bread soaked in milk with a little sugar on top—Christina was getting an education about real life.

With the help of the *Advisor in Sickness and in Health* that stood on the top shelf of the bookcase in Christina's house, the secrets of childbirth were revealed. Unfortunately, the chapter describing "productive intercourse" was not illustrated. That was a real shame, since without pictures neither Christina nor Trudy could quite figure out exactly how the human race managed to reproduce itself.

But Trudy still insisted on taking Christina to walk past the angel-maker's half-hidden front gate. The Nazi Women's Auxiliary would soon put her out of business. After all, Germany needed children. More like cannon fodder, her father would say. Whoever brings a child into the world these days should have his head examined! And with that, he quashed forever Christina's hope that she might still have a sister or brother.

Unfortunately, children have no say in such matters. No one told Christina about the new plan to move, either. They simply informed her after the decision had been made and then couldn't imagine why she was so upset at the prospect of such a wrenching change.

Out to the new subdivision? Why there? Why are we moving at all?

Because this old house belongs to the whole Steiger family, and it's falling apart. Furthermore, your father can't remodel it because his siblings can't agree on what should happen with their share of the property. That's why.

It may be small, but it's all mine, announced Christina's mother as they stood in front of the little house she had bought with the money she'd gotten from selling the last parcel of farmland she had inherited. For the first time, Christina sees her mother in a state that could be called "happy."

The kitchen will be green, light green, oil paint, of course, Herr Zeh. And wallpaper in the living room, good quality, preferably with a small pattern. The painter took note of these instructions. Christina could have a say as well, and said she'd like yellow flowers on a green background. No, that would never do. Pale yellow on a white background. That would be better.

Their new quarters were the right half of a duplex, sharing a firewall with the Klein family, who occupied the other half. The entrance was in the back. From the landing on the stairs, you could see over the wall that divided their yard from the neighbors'. The walls on the second floor angled in slightly, with gable windows on the slanted sides under the hip roof. From the little upstairs balcony, you could see the canal where the *Perle von Hirschhorn* was just then gliding by.

"Ahoy there, Captain Weber! Have a good trip!" Christina shouted. Christina was convinced that Captain Weber would have waved back to her if he hadn't had to keep his hands on the steering wheel while maneuvering out of the way of a tugboat coming the other way.

The house was well situated, no doubt about it. But it smelled completely different.

During her first night in the new house, the water in the canal came up the steps and lapped at the threshold of her room, and Christina sailed away through the yellow anemones on the wallpaper, over the pebbled balcony, heading towards an exotic enchanted land.

She didn't quite get there. She only made it as far as the door to her parents' bedroom, where her father found her and took her into their bed.

When I'm older, Father, then . . . then, let's go away together, some place far away. On the motorcycle.

Of course, Christina, of course we will.

Their home was in a new subdivision. In the twenties, a real estate developer had bought the old Hellwig brick factory site and constructed side-by-side duplexes, offering young working families from the village the opportunity to go into debt.

Owning your own home is a dream come true—that was what they always claimed. But in order to keep that home from being foreclosed during the Depression, families would occupy only a few rooms, bedding down the children in the attic so that they could rent out the rest of the house. Even after times improved somewhat, the renters stayed on, because the extra income made it possible to enlarge the attic, pave the courtyard, and make all sorts of other improvements. Eventually real estate speculators sold off the rest of the lots to city dwellers who wanted to move out to where they could have fancy country houses built.

As a result, the new neighborhood brought together city folks and villagers, rich and poor, a grouping that was difficult for the grown-ups. The children, not yet aware of social standing, had it a little easier, at least in the beginning. The kids played in the street, since there was only bicycle traffic. Christina knew most of them, at least by sight, since they all attended the village school. At first, she shyly hung back in her yard watching them play until someone waved to her to come join the game.

They were playing the chimney sweep game, and Christina was drafted to play the role of the dog. She crept along on all fours and made barking noises, trying her best to sound like a dog. She knew that you had to suffer a few indignities in order to overcome the embarrassment that was part of this initiation ceremony. She'd done it all before.

Later they showed her the hiding place under the canal bridge where the club had their secret meetings. Just before dark they'd go down Uferstrasse to grocer Geiss's yard, which was always full of cardboard boxes. They'd pretend that the boxes were the water, diving into the sea of cardboard cartons, pretending to fight with each other. And as the anglers returned from the river, they'd taunt them, hardly able to control their laughter, chanting *No fish today, no fish today, they're biting but they got away!*

This was Christina's world: to the right, the canal, to the left, the river, and further down, the lock behind which the canal and the river merged again to flow into the Rhine. It was the world she'd later call home, a term not so much for the place as for the people who were there, at a time when nothing had yet been determined, when everything was still possible.

People like Gerda Martin, Christina's bosom buddy, who lived across from her on the ground floor below the Bohrers, and who, early each morning, put notes into Christina's mailbox that divided up the day into the hours they'd spend with and without each other. She was Christina's first true friend, and as a token of their friendship, she let Gerda be the first to write in her new poetry album:

> *I claim my place, dear friend of mine,*
> *This last page in your book of rhyme,*
> *Now no one can come after me,*
> *And claim your better friend to be.*

Gerda always smelled of Palmolive soap, because her chores—either cleaning or serving customers—required her to continually wash her hands. She worked in the family business. Her father, Fritz, had apprenticed as a plasterer, but when he turned out to have a pathological aversion to getting his hands dirty, he felt he had no choice but to go into sales. He did not go door to door—that he adamantly refused to do. But he had a wife who could peddle his wares from their washhouse (temporarily outfitted with shelves for this purpose), and a daughter who could help out and who could deliver ice during the summer and coal during the winter. If his wife and daughter didn't hustle, he could sometimes become abusive. But when things were going well and there was money in the till, he was transformed into a father who was the envy of all the other children in the neighborhood. He decorated his little back yard with Chinese lanterns and personally served his guests his homemade lemon sherbet. Afterwards, accompanying himself on his accordion, he would sing the latest hit tunes. "Star of Rio, You Are My Destiny"—this was his favorite song ever since he had become infatuated with La Jana, the exotic dancer and film actress.

According to village gossip, she was not the only one he was taken with. There were other, less exotic objects of his fancy, such as Frau Sack.

She lived with her paraplegic husband and his generous disability pension in their large house at the end of Hindenburgstrasse and was quite reclusive, until one day she accepted Fritz Martin's repeated invitation to attend one of his Chinese lantern parties. Ever since, Fritz had spent many an evening sitting on the Sacks' balcony, comforting this poor, unfortunate woman. Gerda often had the thankless task of going over there to fetch her father. While carrying out one of these missions at her mother's insistence, Mrs. Sack had snippily turned Gerda away at the front gate, causing the usually good-natured Gerda to sock Mrs. Sack. That brought Gerda a good licking, but made her, in Christina's opinion, a fighter for justice.

Gerda avoided her father for days until he remorsefully abandoned Mrs. Sack to her fate. Gerda, in her girlish innocence, believed that from now on everything would get better.

Hmm, I'm not so sure about that, said Elise, who felt very sorry for poor Emma Martin and her daughter. She therefore bought her coffee and her yarn from them, even though she could have gotten them cheaper in the village. But it really bothered her that, by doing so, she was also supporting that adulterous bastard. Don't repeat that, Christina, she said.

Christina's father, who was in the habit of judging everyone based on their previous party affiliation, sometimes even defended his former Red comrade Fritz. But in such matters, Elise could have cared less about party membership, whether Conservative, Nazi, or Communist. An adulterous bastard was an adulterous bastard.

Even though Christina was good at sniffing out Commies, she would not have thought of Herr Martin as one of them. On the other hand, Herr Haas, the vegetable man who always parked his three-wheeled Hanomag motorcycle in front of the Steiger's house when he offered his wares on Hindenburgstrasse—"POTATOES, LET-TUCE, CUUUUCUMBERS!"—was a Commie for sure. Christina's mother, thanks to her backyard garden, could supply her own vegetables and saw no need to purchase anything from Herr Haas.

We can pretty well take care of ourselves, she boasted through the recently constructed espalier of fruit trees to her neighbor, Frau Späther. Frau Späther's garden completely contradicted Elise's favorite saying: "No weeds allowed!"

But sometimes, if Christina's father happened to be home when Herr Haas was out front haggling with his customers about produce, Philipp would send her out to ask Herr Haas if he had bananas, oranges, or lemons. Herr Haas always took notice of her as soon as she stepped out of the doorway but waited until his last customer had left before answering, and his answer was always quite specific. For example: next Thursday at four o'clock. Christina was sharp enough to realize that the exchange had nothing to do with tropical fruit. She was also clever enough to know not to ask any questions when her father had her deliver a bag with unknown contents to Herr Liebig's laundry in the neighboring village, having given her specific instructions that she was to hand over the package to no one but Herr Liebig himself.

One time, when she was deep in a game of marbles that had already cost her half of her collection, she had left one of these mysterious bags at the side of the road and forgotten about it. By the time she remembered what she was supposed to do on her secret mission, the bag had disappeared.

Words cannot describe the kind of fear and horror Christina now felt. She was so terrified that she wanted to throw up, which she did when she got as far as Tante Lisa's front yard. Wanting to die, right there next to her aunt's ornamental spruce tree, wanting to leave this world, she kept asking herself just how she would accomplish that. All she could think of was that ever since last November the package deliveries had become more and more frequent. The bags also now came in various colors and, just like her marble sack, were lighter, so light that they could be blown away by a sudden gust of wind and end up against the Bohrer's garden fence. Which is where Christina finally found the missing bag after having looked for it everywhere.

Under the canal bridge she untied the string at the opening and took out the piece of paper inside. On it was written the names of people who had been arrested. She recognized only one of them, Otto Frank, the ironmonger in town who supplied her father's construction business and who had once given Christina a pair of ice skates at Christmas. A Jew. So that was it! She carefully put the piece of paper back in the bag and set out for the Liebig laundry.

It was drizzling this November day, as it most likely had on the day when what later became known in history books as "Kristall-nacht"[8]—"The Night of the Broken Glass"—had taken place.

On this particular morning, Christina was on her way to the streetcar she took every day to get to her school in town. As usual, she walked along the main street with her head down. Although they had long tried to break her of that habit, she found that she liked looking down while walking, and more often than not she would find a marble, a coin, once even a gold bracelet. It wasn't real gold, but still….

Suddenly she began to notice shards of glass, and when she looked up, she saw a crowd congregating on Judenstrasse around some furniture and other household goods. There was a lot of pushing and pulling, everyone wanting to get their hands on something. Tante Greta was among them and was arguing with a woman over a chair, a particularly nice chair that—thanks to Tante Lisa's expert knowledge of period furniture—would enter family lore as the "Louis XIV chair." Christina slunk along close to the fronts of the houses, but there wasn't much to see through the broken window-panes. The rooms had been completely emptied out: nothing was left but a few pieces of clothing lying on the floor. No one lived here any longer. All the doors were standing open.

The people who had lived here were now sitting in the back of a truck in front of City Hall. An elderly man who stared blankly into the distance, and two women with snow-white hair. One of them had a blanket around her shoulders; the other, in a black dress with her arms folded in front of her, was noticeably cold. One might assume that Christina hesitated briefly before moving on. Perhaps she thought momentarily of those gold stars with which she had been rewarded throughout her childhood. But putting such humane

---

[8] November 9, 1938.

thoughts into spontaneous action would have meant having to hand over her brand-new hand-knit dirndl jacket to a stranger on the truck and then be cold herself. That would have been too much to expect of a young girl, even one who had been brought up to always be kind and helpful to old people.

Besides, as was later reported, it wasn't actually a truck, but rather an ambulance that was taking the old people to a nursing home, so that in the end Christina's version of the whole episode was attributed to her vivid imagination.

But I swear it's true, cross my heart! She had seen the whole thing with her very own eyes, as she told Waldemar after sprinting to catch up to him on the bridge.

Jewish rabble, is all he said, uttered with a trace of masculine superiority, in contrast to the obvious sympathy felt by his out-of-breath companion.

In school, the whole thing was explained as a spontaneous reaction of the German people against the Jews. Fräulein Rast, PhD, the fifth grade's homeroom teacher at the Elizabeth Gymnasium, also took it upon herself to bring up the topic of racial inferiority.

That evening, Christina tried to discuss this newly acquired knowledge with her parents. She was immediately silenced, since in this house there would be no talk of racial inferiority. And besides, there were things needing immediate attention, in particular a certain Louis XIV chair that was the catalyst for one of the most intense family debates ever—one that turned into a feud between brother and sister and ended up with Christina being forbidden to ever again set foot in her Tante Greta's house.

When her father learned that his very own sister had helped herself to property belonging to someone else, he had felt obliged to march her, along with the chair, back down the main street (he dragged her, according to Tante Eva) to put the thing back where it belonged, namely in the living room of the widow Kahn. It was like running the gauntlet, Christina's mother confided while they were drying the dishes. If only Greta had not gotten involved. If only! Had she not, her brother Philipp would have attended the funeral of this sister, who only six months later dropped dead of a stroke on that very same street, leaving behind her husband, the volunteer fire-chief, and almost the entire family to mourn her death.

"No matter what you expect, it'll be something else"—Elise's favorite saying, always hoping for the best but anticipating something terrible. Forever the prognosticator, pointlessly predicting the worst. Was she always innocent of the disasters that she envisaged?

For instance, she is convinced that Christina will not learn anything worthwhile by continuing on into the upper grades of the Gymnasium. She noticed right away that Christina's interaction with the "upper class girls" was changing her daughter in a way she couldn't quite explain.

"Pride goeth before a fall," she warned Christina, who lately had been acting like a prima donna. For example, she did not like to be disturbed while doing her homework, even when her mother suddenly realized that she needed bread from the bakery. It was also unheard of that a Gymnasium student be expected to wear sleeve protectors. Even worse, she started speaking High German rather than the local dialect that was laughed at by her classmates and frowned upon by her teacher. When she started asking for "marmalade" for her bread at breakfast instead of calling it jam like everyone else in the village, her mother announced that she was not going to put up with any more such nonsense.

It's not easy when, for the first time, you are confronted with natural self-confidence, the innate property of the well-to-do. This confidence did not come naturally to Christina, who kept getting hung up at every turn. Driven by a fierce pride, she painstakingly managed to catch up to her classmates academically, but it was more complicated than that. She simply lacked the self-assurance that the others had acquired over the years. They were somebodies, and they knew it.

Their fancy homes on the east side of town or out in the suburbs—the big, multi-storied houses and the mothers who were never at home—these were just the outward signs of her classmates' inherent belief that they were somehow better than other people.

Let in by a servant, who immediately knew that she was dealing with an upstart, Christina was shown into the children's quarters. There was tea and cake—and sugar cubes—she would report when she got home. For Christina, sugar cubes were reserved for special occasions, such as birthdays or family celebrations. What she does not report is what happened once again to demonstrate her lack of certain social graces.

Sugar tongs: an instrument designed for the specific purpose of transferring a sugar cube into a teacup without one's hand touching the cube. Unaware of this, Christina, practical by nature, picked up the sugar cube with her fingers and carefully inserted it into the silver tongs, then let it plop into the teacup, causing a pained silence among the company assembled at the table.

But her faux pas had in fact been duly noted, and later, during recess, she learned that her hostess, Martha Stein, had immediately related the whole scene in great detail to the entire fifth grade, resulting in general amusement about what came to be known as "Christina's sugar tongs episode."

In her diary, the victim quoted Goethe: *Be steadfast against those who oppose you, call on the gods for their aid!*

The gods did not come immediately to her rescue, but Tante Lisa did. Always concerned about Christina's manners, she tutored her niece in the ways one should conduct oneself in "good company." But that was not really enough when you had parents, in particular a father who was determined to be, and remain, unmannered. He was the sort who would stand around in his moleskin pants, spotted from top to bottom with food stains, devouring a piece of cake while interrupting your coffee foursome with your girlfriends. Then he'd thank the girls for coming over, since in their honor, for a change there would be toilet paper in the bathroom. Otherwise, he'd say, he'd have to make do with a page from the *Swastika Herald*—though it was a paper whose headlines were perfect for wiping one's behind. During the ensuing silence, he would blithely continue to munch on his cake while Christina died of embarrassment. You can't get rid of your parents or exchange them for a new set; you can only pretend, now and then, that they don't exist.

Feigning deep regret, Christina told her classmates that unfortunately her birthday party—an event that required one to issue invitations to school friends—would only be a small family affair this year because her mother was suffering from a heart ailment, and the doctor had insisted on limiting the number of visitors. Having a mother who suffered from a medical condition sounded rather sophisticated, since "suffering" wasn't the same thing as actually being sick. Tante Eva, for example, was sick with diabetes. She worked more slowly than the others during the potato harvest and often had to lie down in the afternoon, so that frequently she didn't have supper ready when the menfolk came home from work. Gudrun Lindermann's mother, on the other hand, was a woman who "suffered." She spent summers in a sanatorium in the Black Forest. Otherwise she almost always just sat around with her hands in her lap, usually in the sunroom of the Lindermann house, and "suffered." From the waist down she was always wrapped in a pastel-colored blanket, which led Christina to wonder if she even had legs.

But she did, a fact that became abundantly clear later on when the Lindermann house was hit by a firebomb during an air-raid. Then Christina saw Frau Lindermann running back and forth between the smoking ruins and the small truck into which she had placed her remaining valuables, covering them with one of those very same pastel blankets.

But for now, the war was still a long way off. Keeping the peace in Europe was something near and dear to the Führer's heart. Fräulein Rast, PhD, who taught German and History, knew what she was talking about. She admired the Führer with as much fervor as she admired Alarich, the King of the Goths.

In honor of the Führer, she led the fifth grade in celebrating Germany's triumphal march into Czechoslovakia, an event that was not celebrated at Christina's house. At home, they turned off the radio rather than listen to his fiery speech in September 1938. In Christina's house, every evening between ten and eleven, her parents listened to the short-wave radio tuned to 29.8, the *Free Germany* station: Down with Hitler's dictatorship! Long live peace! All the while Christina sat in bed with the blanket over her knees reading Herta Biedermann's *Guide for the League of German Girls*[9] by flashlight.

I'm going to go join up, Christina announced the following Saturday, already halfway out the door, hoping that the words "join up" would fade away before they reached the kitchen.

Join up? She heard it shouted from the kitchen window, a statement that was half question, half surprise, but that ended up with an official declaration: Don't you dare!

Christina pretended she hadn't heard and rode her bike to the Hitler Youth Clubhouse where the ten-year-old initiates were already gathered around the woman who was giving instructions about how they should form up.

---

[9] The *Bund Deutscher Mädel*, the girls' wing of the Hitler Youth.

Count off! One, two, three! Rows of three, forward, march!

Singing the *Horst-Wessel-Lied*, they marched down Schlossstrasse, past Schmidt's barbershop, where her father got a shave every Saturday afternoon (therefore, keep your eyes to the left, if he sees you, it's all over!), all the way to the sports field, around the field to the end, then "Halt!"

She's in Group 2, and the leader's name is Titti. Titti lives on Schillerstrasse, across the canal where the townspeople are gradually buying up the empty lots and having her father build them their big houses.

Christina can't resist mentioning, ever so subtly, that she knows which house Titti lives in, since she had often brought her father's thermos of tea to the building site when the house was under construction. Covered entrance on the left, red facing brick, brown tiled roof, right?

Titti seems impressed, and the village girls are also surprised. When they start swinging the Indian clubs, Christina is allowed to step out in front of the group and show off her talent for rhythmic movement. It's as if she's sprouted wings; all of a sudden she feels like she's above the others who start to mimic her circular movements swinging the club. Not until she's on her way home does she come back down to earth and begin to have second thoughts.

What does a girl do when she doesn't dare go home? She goes over to Tante Eva's, waters the garden, feeds the chickens, brings up beer from the cellar, and makes herself generally indispensable, just in case her parents won't let her into the house. But they do.

Where were you all this time? At the sports field.

Her mother gives her one of those we'll-talk-about-it-later looks, and Christina knows it will be a conversation just between the two of them, since under no circumstances may her father ever find out that she has gone over to the enemy camp.

Fräulein Rast, however, may know, wants to know, has to know about it, since she is a teacher, a woman with political ambition who feels duty bound to instill in her pupils a new worldview. Her watchword is "community," and any bit of individuality, any action that hinted at any aspect of selfishness, is immediately noted and censured. Since Christina knows that she is suspected of having a mind of her own, she naturally tries extra hard to fit in with the others. But her classmates don't make it easy on her. No matter how much she seeks their approval, she always comes up short. She knows that she needs to make a good impression, but she can never quite pull it off.

But necessity is the mother of invention. What you don't know, for example, you have to look up. So, in order to look things up, you buy a pocket encyclopedia, which she does at Guckenmus's bookstore, where she can charge her purchases. In order to make an impression, she decides to buy two notebooks and six erasers, which she hands out to the classmates who are there with her in the bookstore. They are delighted—or at least Christina interprets the looks on their faces as delight. But the look on her father's face as he waved the bill under her nose was another matter entirely. She stared at his architect's license, hanging in its black frame on the wall behind him, reading each of the names of the licensing committee while she let the torrent of words roll over her.

He didn't need six erasers in a whole year! She didn't either. But how could she ever explain to him that six erasers could move mountains and open doors that up until now had been closed to her?

Her mother, who had not been particularly enthusiastic about her daughter going on to Gymnasium in the first place, took this fresh opportunity to jump in and get off her chest her thoughts about the crazy ideas the girl had gotten into her head lately.

Christina let it all go in one ear and out the other. She'd heard it all before. She was tempted to tell them both to go to the devil!— but years of being taught to be respectful kept her from saying anything. What could she do? The only thing was to fervently promise, once again, to do better. Her brain probably had good reason to store such promises in its short-term memory, since they were constantly being overwritten.

Christina got a "Very Good" on her class essay titled "The Leap off the Canal Bridge." At that point, she hoped it might indeed be possible for her to become the person her teacher wanted her to be.

In any case, according to Titti, she has leadership ability, and they want her to become a coach for the southern chapter of the League of German Girls. At their training camp, which at home is simply referred to under the code name of "summer camp," they want to prepare her for this most esteemed position. Her strong suits were apparently in rhythmic clapping and in the hundred-meter dash, since running cross-country gives her a side stitch, something which, according to the camp leader, is caused by improper breathing. She has absolutely no talent for making her bed, and thus gets demerits every morning at rollcall. In the Ravensbrück concentration camp people got fifteen lashes with the whip for not making their bed properly, but Christina didn't know that.

Despite such shortcomings, she's ready for the job by the time her training ends. Of course, in order to do the job properly, one needs a proper uniform, but her mother is not prepared to invest twelve marks in the blue skirt, white button-up blouse, and neckerchief with leather clasp that would enable her daughter to join the leadership ranks. Besides, back in '32 Elise had carried a banner at a German Communist Party rally, and that was not so easily forgotten. At the time, Thälmann had urged his party brothers and sisters to take action against the Fascists, and on the day before Hitler assumed power, Elise herself had ridden her bicycle through the villages passing out leaflets. That was our last attempt, Christina, to turn back the tide. And besides, what would your father say if he found out? Things like this get around. Had she forgotten that as a child she had marched around the kitchen with her fists raised, singing *Roter Wedding*,[10] while her father looked on approvingly, then picked her up and made her giggle—his little Communist girl! Was this the same Christina who now seemed ready to betray her political heritage?

So, no uniform, no illustrious career, just an ordinary member of the League of German Girls who had to show up and play her part so that she didn't get expelled from school. She would have to be satisfied with that.

At home she continued to be the obedient daughter. The transformation of the obedient daughter into the League member took place each Saturday afternoon. She ran down back alleys to join the group of faithfuls who had been instructed to prepare for the upcoming sports competition. Spurred on by high expectations, Christina sought new ways to satisfy her need for approval. She trained nonstop. She ran her feet raw on the new cinder track at the sports field. Always keeping her sights on the finish line, she took off from her hand-dug starting pits like a rocket, knowing that, as her coach had impressed on her, at the start every second counts.

Christina takes off and imagines overtaking all the others. Among them is Martha, whose running pants flap around her spindly legs, as well as Isolde Brümmer, the top student in their class, who suffers from asthma and wheezes as she tries to catch up with Christina. But she is not to be overtaken. She breathes deeply, lengthens her stride in a final burst of speed, and throws herself into the tape at the finish line, knowing she has won. Christina is in training.

You should have been there to see it, the ceremony at which the silver victory pin was awarded to the winner! Christina was now a winner, and as befitting a winner, she accepted the congratulations of her comrades with appropriate modesty. Only when Fräulein Rast in-

---

[10] The unofficial anthem of the Communist ("Red") Front, referring to "Red" Wedding, a working-class section of Berlin.

troduced her to the class as the victor did she have to restrain herself from bragging about her success. Bravo, Christina! The pin was passed around and admired, while its owner basked in the group's admiration. It was only at home that not a single word was said about it. Instead, the victor got slapped because she had forgotten to go to the shop after school to pick up the blueprints her father urgently needed.

This slap stung her for the next several days, and no matter how much she cried, her tears couldn't extinguish the pain. She should just let it go; he hadn't really meant it. But he had meant it. Maybe he suspected that she really did want to be part of this cadre, that she really enjoyed the camaraderie of this new circle of friends?

Christina was confused, and despite her best efforts, she just couldn't figure it out. She knew that it wouldn't be easy to give up what she had worked so hard to achieve. But she thought about it a lot, especially when, once again, her father didn't return after being summoned to Gestapo headquarters.

Whenever her father was gone, they had hot cereal and stewed fruit for dinner, Christina's favorite meal. But this time, she couldn't eat a thing. She had a stomachache. Even Tante Eva's peppermint tea didn't help. When her father came home after two days of interrogation, things had progressed to cold compresses and oatmeal baths, and the feverish patient had sunk into a kind of delirium.

She tosses and turns from one side to the other, from the wallpaper with yellow anemones to the window whose drawn white curtains obstruct her view of the cherry tree outside. She wants to see the tree because if the leaves are out, then everything will be fine—something she knew from a story about a sick girl who had to wait through the whole long winter for the leaves to come out on the trees before she could get better. Without such signs, it would be unbearable for children to be sick.

The cherry tree not only has leaves, but is heavy with fruit, and Christina tightly grasps her father's hand after he opens the window—because he can tell what she wants just by looking at her. She loves him dearly, although she doesn't yet understand that you can't make demands of love. She is not prepared to accept him just as he is. She wants him to change, a sin she will commit over and over again, often with her mother's blessing.

She finally feels well enough to go see Dr. Hoffman during his office hours. His office is on the ground floor of his house, a building set well back from the street near the old castle grounds. In the graveled front yard there's a chestnut tree and a bicycle rack that's full to overflowing, meaning that today there will undoubtedly be a long wait.

Even in mid-summer the waiting room is cool. Dr. Hoffman's hands are even colder as he pokes around at various places on Christina's body, trying to elicit a reaction. Does it hurt there?

Nothing hurts when you're lying on the examining table. Her mother tries to help the doctor by showing him the place that most recently had caused Christina the most pain. He presses harder until she winces.

Aha! the doctor says, as his mustached upper lip broadens into a smile that makes him look amazingly like Willy Birgel, the movie actor. This may be the reason Dr. Hoffman is such strong competition for old Dr. Müller. The village women swear by Dr. Hoffman. The man really knows his stuff! Christina will also attest to his skill a year later, when he stitches up her left underarm after she has been bitten by the Rottweiler who belonged to Herr Bühler, the baker. At the moment, however, he pronounces her stomachache the result of an infection in her stomach lining, an impressive diagnosis. He prescribes a bland diet and Baldrian drops for her nerves.

Elise can't believe her ears. Something for her nerves? Is that even possible for someone her age? Elise is no doubt thinking of Herr

Glaser, a teacher who had recently been relieved of his duties, who went around waving his arms about, white spittle in the corners of his mouth, conversing with imaginary people about the great number of sinners in the village. Now there was somebody who had a problem with his nerves!

Elise manages to pull herself together and only later, still upset by this latest stroke of fate, does she collapse into Oma Stina's antimacassar-bedecked upholstered chair, her face in her hands.

Such things ought to be discussed only within the bosom of the family. And even there, some family members are more comforting than others. For Elise, it had always been her mother, a woman who never considered bad luck to be something personal but rather one of life's inevitable trials, something one could best withstand on a full stomach. She brings out a huge loaf of bread and some ham from the kitchen along with a jar of homemade pickles, gets a bottle of red wine from the cellar, and sits her eldest daughter down for a meal. Oma Stina's ever-increasing girth testified to a life filled with trials.

For Christina, it was her Tante Eva who had always been the most comforting. You could let yourself into her house and immediately know everything she had cooked and done that week. The house would smell like fried potatoes, garden soil, and the goose pen. Sometimes even like the carbide she used to fill her husband's bicycle lamp before she went to bed, so that he'd be able to find his way back home after his night out on the town. Onkel Thomas staggered home quite often. Sometimes he got completely lost. Then the village pubs and the neighborhood would have to be searched. After the last church festival, they found him under the new bridge over the autobahn. He was looking for rabbit food, he explained with a thick tongue.

At four o'clock in the morning? Christina didn't think it was right for Tante Eva to have to accept such an excuse. She didn't understand that it was not a matter of truthfulness, but rather the need for a woman to come to terms with a life that she was powerless to change.

Christina believed in change. She noticed that she herself was changing. There was evidence of something going on that even an outgrown undershirt couldn't contain. Then there was her mother telling her that she shouldn't run around the house half naked and that she was a little too old to be romping around in her father's bed on Sunday mornings.

Either you're too young or you're too old to do whatever it is you're wanting to do. Isn't that right, Tante Eva?

Her aunt nodded in agreement and handed her the mixing bowl to lick, once more breaching one of the barriers that a girl at the advanced age of eleven begins to erect around herself.

Elise had never understood what it was that attracted her daughter to the house on Ringstrasse. Although Eva was indeed a good soul, Elise had never felt quite comfortable in her sister-in-law's house. For one thing, it needed a good cleaning. She should just offer to help Eva do it, since housekeeping was clearly not her forte. No doubt about it, Eva's house was a total mess.

Elise's house was a model of order; there the sofa pillows were always plumped and neatly aligned in a row. Every other Monday was washday. On Tuesdays it was ironing and mending. During the week things were dusted and, on Friday, everything thoroughly cleaned.

Twice a year there was a major housecleaning, when the mattresses and carpets were dragged outside and beaten till the dust rose up to the second story balcony, where it then floated back in through the open windows.

Inside the house, order reigned supreme. Only Christina's room was an eyesore to a proper housewife like Elise. Christina's room looked like someplace where Polacks lived, though you had to take such an expression with a grain of salt because it was highly unlikely that Elise had ever laid eyes on a Polish home. She had not been farther east than Nuremberg—the German Workers' Association Gymnastics Club had held a convention there once. She had traveled around the southwestern part of the country while she was working for an upper-class family who moved a lot and who took Elise, the best maid they had ever had, along with them. She had been the smartest one in her family, but because she was the eldest and her father had died young, she could not take up an apprenticeship and had to earn money instead. She worked first in a grenade factory during the war, and then, as already mentioned, as a maid. As she never failed to mention.

She had had to sacrifice herself for the good of her six younger siblings. When she talked about her childhood memories, her voice lost its usual shrill tone and made her daughter feel for her, a daughter who could never fully understand what unfulfilled dreams and hopes her mother harbored deep within herself.

At moments like this, mother and daughter should have been able to establish a connection; Christina should have been able to overcome her fear of never being able to please her mother, should have been able to take her mother's hand as it moved mechanically back and forth over the table top, sweeping up crumbs that she then put in her apron pocket. This was the bird food her mother would later sprinkle out on the windowsill to lure the shy birds from their hiding places. Luring her daughter out of her hiding places was more than Elise was ready or able to do. The birds, however, came gladly to her and made a mess in the yard and on the balcony, until the Steigers built a large aviary with double doors close to the washhouse. There her mother would sit, working on her mending or embroidery, and imitating the finches' or canaries' chirping until the whole flock would gather, perch on the wires, and sing with her.

Christina thought that the birds really wanted to be free, but her mother, the president of this bird society, knew better. They were lucky to have it so good.

Even luckier was the fledgling stork that fell out of the nest up on the chimney of the old tile factory. For a while it could only flop around in the open field, waiting for the neighborhood children to provide its daily ration of frogs—which required considerable personal commitment. Christina discovered where the frogs could be found but was never successful in catching these long-legged brown or green amphibians. Catching the frogs was the responsibility of some of the others, like Ossie Späther, for example, who always carried things like spiders, toads, bugs, and once, even a slow-worm, in his pockets—not because he wanted to frighten the others, but because he really was fond of these creatures. Ossie was elected the Frog King and was allowed to christen the stork. He got the name Hannibal from Christina, who knew that Hannibal, like the stork, had come from North Africa.

Hannibal ad portas! This ancient Roman call-to-arms now found its way from Christina's Latin class to the neighborhood and remained the password of the Canal Club kids long after Hannibal, at first quite reluctantly, took his place among his fellow flock-mates heading south.

Hannibal would return the following spring and settle into a nest in the steeple of the Lutheran church. But he remained a bachelor, probably because no lady stork wanted to brood her young next to the newly installed siren on top of City Hall. No matter that it was only supposed to be used for drills: the wail of the siren was bloodcurdling.

Hannibal ad portas! rings out under the canal bridge. Christina hoists herself up the cable that runs the length of the cement slope to the platform nestled in the bridge pillars. The others are already sitting there in candlelight, and nimble-fingered Ossie is casting sil-houettes on the wall. A rabbit's head with long floppy ears becomes a butterfly, a porcupine slowly stiffens its bristles, and then, in the middle of the guessing game, somebody utters the loaded words that no one wants to hear: There's going to be war!

War. Nobody has to look this word up in the dictionary, since they already know about it from the last one. Onkel Seppel, Father's brother, died in it. Christina knows of him from the enlarged picture in Tante Eva's parlor, where with his watery eyes he takes part in all the family gatherings. His wife, the Wagners' daughter Erna, had sup-posedly leapt out of bed screaming her husband's name at exactly the moment a flamethrower at Verdun transformed him into a field-grey torch. According to Tante Eva, that was a kind of telepathy that was said to occur quite often.

Christina would have liked to know what kind of thoughts were being transferred that way, but this is not a question to ask Lina Fuchs, no matter how often you go to her little drygoods shop for thread, zippers, or rick-rack, especially if Frau Althaus, the seam-stress, is there. Even Frau Althaus, who goes door to door in her trade and therefore knows everything about everybody, knows only that Lina has just never gotten over her loss.

Lina must have lost somebody, no doubt about it. More than twenty years later, she's still laying flowers at the war memo-rial, always at night so that no one will see her. Christina thinks that's romantic.

The next chance she gets, she decides to take some pansies to the war memorial and read all the names engraved on the black basalt monument. She has to use her barrette to dig out the moss that's growing in the letters, particularly in those of Onkel Seppel's name: Joseph Steiger, 1898 – 1917. Further questions about the war brought other long-forgotten memories to the surface. Opa Berry, for example, initially survived a gunshot wound to his lung, but succumbed to it right after the armistice, leaving behind a grieving widow and seven children. His picture hangs in Oma Stina's bedroom, the frame draped in black crepe. There he stands with his hand on his uniform belt, his bayonet half concealed by his left arm, leaning a little forward with his right hand on the back of a chair in front of a curtain drawn to the right, behind which stands a pillar entwined with exotic leaves and flowers.

Christina's father had also been in that war, but only at the very end when it was all but lost.

Our Führer, of course, also fought and suffered a poison gas attack, for which he was awarded the Iron Cross, which he always proudly wears on his breast pocket. Waldemar is showing off again with what he knows about the Führer. And because he has forgotten his student bus pass and doesn't want to have to pay, he starts holding forth about the Treaty of Versailles so that the conductor won't dare interrupt him to ask for his ticket. That's what Waldemar is counting on.

Oh yes, the Treaty of Versailles, that treaty that imposed total ruin on the German people; the treaty that the Führer wants and intends to free us from. The people are no longer silently suffering humiliation and dishonor. *Because today Germany hears us, and tomorrow, the whole world!*

War is at our doorstep! Now it's okay to talk about that, since "Poland's army is ready to attack." "Battle-ready Polish troops amassing at their western borders," and "Tank attack on Danzig planned." These are headlines in the *Swastika Herald*, copies of which hang from clothespins in the windows flanking Fat Trudy's kiosk. Business is good today. The German people are reading about the Führer's solution for a peaceful revision of the Eastern Border question and his recommendation for the administration of the Danzig Corridor, as well as resolution of the German-Polish minority issue. The situation is such that any further incident might lead to unleashing the military forces that both sides have in place.

Trudy was of the opinion that things would blow over, but then ended up doing something uncharacteristic for an astute businesswoman such as herself: She handed her faithful customer Christina her sausage, as usual with extra mustard, but this time gave it to her for free.

Enjoy it, my little one, who knows . . . ?

No one seemed to grasp the fact that things were about to come to a head. Gone was the urgent desire, palpable in early summer, to relax and enjoy life. At that point, everyone wanted to do something quickly before it was too late. In order to satisfy Christina's long-standing wish to see something of the outside world, a trip to the Black Forest was planned. To accomplish this, the old Opel motorcycle had to be tuned up. The passenger footrests were raised up for Christina, and during a test ride, she had to learn how to properly lean into curves and hold on tight. Her mother had second thoughts about the whole thing. She knew from experience that whenever Philipp got on a straight stretch he tried to coax out everything that the engine had to offer. But so far, he had never had an accident, and that ended up being the deciding factor. Tante Lisa scrounged up a pair of goggles for Christina, who sometimes wore them when she was riding her bicycle just so she could get used to them, or so she said. Just to show off, her friends said somewhat enviously. Nevertheless, they all showed up to wish her well at five o'clock in the morning in front of the Steiger house on the day Christina and her father were leaving. Tante Eva stuffed an extra packet of goodies into Christina's rucksack and predicted they'd have good weather, because whenever angels travel, the heavens smile.

There was a lot of traffic on the autobahn. Columns of army vehicles clogged the lanes, but luckily, they got off at the Rastatt interchange and headed east.

It was wonderful, she would later claim quite emphatically as she passed around the photo album, the snapshots mounted with black triangular corners to keep them in place. That's Freudenstadt. And here's the Mummelsee in the heart of the Black Forest. That's Father and me at the Swiss border, with the German border guard making sure that no German, particularly anyone eligible for the draft, foregoes the opportunity to serve the Fatherland. Only later did her mother bring up the question of whether her father might have toyed with such an idea—of just leaving everything behind and emigrating. She'd have told him he could leave, but it would be without her and Christina. In any case, he stayed. In the picture taken at the border, he stands in his brown leather riding gear with his goggles pushed up on his forehead, a little off to the side of Christina and the border guard, but by no means looking like he was thinking of fleeing. It was just that he had set the camera for a delayed exposure and barely managed to sprint from the tripod into the picture in time.

It really was great. Even her classmates found Christina's photos fantastic, particularly the one of her sitting on the driver's seat leaning over the gas tank, holding on to the Opel's handlebars. Okay, the bike was up on its kickstand, but so what? As soon as she got back, her teacher, who had only reluctantly agreed to let Christina be absent from school, made it clear that she'd have to immediately make up all the schoolwork she had missed. The teacher thought they really ought to have postponed the trip until the upcoming summer vacation.

But nothing was postponed in the summer of '39. Nobody was saving money anymore, either. Even Tante Anna decided she could afford to take a vacation for the first time in her life. She sent Tante Eva a postcard from the Spessart in Bavaria with greetings to the entire family. The change of scenery would do her good, she wrote, and the food at the little hotel was ample and quite tasty. At the beginning of June, Tante Lisa went with her son, Ernst August, to her in-laws in Schwerin. Onkel Werner had not been able to accompany them, since he worked as a buyer in the brown-coal industry, and so much was going on at the time with regard to the rationing of critical fuel. We've got to be prepared for the worst-case scenario, he explained to Philipp, who at every opportunity was ready to assume the worst. Those politicians in Berlin are leading us toward catastrophe.

There were late-afternoon debates on the garden bench with Onkel Werner and her father trying to out-smoke each other, blowing smoke rings for Christina, who tried to catch them—and also catch their every word about everything bad about to happen. You're getting us all so worked up, Philipp, warned her mother, with her eye on the espaliered fruit tree behind which the neighbor, Herr Späther, might be listening. But Philipp would not be cut short by his wife and thundered on at length. Those warmongers have been itching for this for years, and now we'll pay the price! No one had believed him when he predicted that this would only lead to disaster.

Onkel Werner seemed to concede the point, since he had nothing by way of a rebuttal. Oma Stina, however, who had wanted to be on her way for an hour but had tarried at the garden gate because she always enjoyed hearing men engaged in a good argument, put in her two-cents worth: It was she who had first spied the thrips in the ripening grain and who had warned that that was a bad omen. It had been just the same in '28, when those insects had ruined the entire crop, and then later in the fall, seven people had drowned in the river after falling through the rotten boards on the deck of a ferry that was not carrying a life boat.

Bad things never happen one at a time. Oma Stina finally took her leave. Enjoy the rest of the evening, everybody! That was how they parted.

Christina's father is sitting at his drafting board and, within the circle of light from the lamp suspended above, drawing in ink the front and side elevations of a house that will never be built. His left eye blinks nervously, and the twitching extends to the corner of his mouth, distorting that side of his face into a grimace that he tries to hide with his hand.

Christina would have liked to ask him a question but knows she mustn't disturb him when he is working. Only if you abide by this rule are you allowed to do your homework at his desk.

Her mother, on the other hand, is allowed to interrupt him because it's time to eat. The usual sounds of the evening can be heard through the open kitchen window. The geese come honking back from the river, and Frau Späther throws them their feed in case their daily catch has not been what than they had hoped for. It never was. Flapping their wings, they attack the kernels of grain, while the clucking chickens retreat into their coop. Herr Klein helps his wife take down the patio umbrella. Herr Heiselbetz whistles to call his children, and the bell of the Brother Conrad Chapel sounds the call to evening vespers.

Her father smacks as he eats. Her mother slices more bread and starts in on the topic of war. Always the practical one, she wants to know whether they really shouldn't buy the air-raid protection devices that have been advertised in the newspaper. Lisa, who buys up everything that's not yet rationed, has already equipped her windows with blackout shades. You never know. It's better to be prepared.

Christina's father does not respond to these suggestions. As far as he's concerned, whenever it starts—and that won't be long now—air-raid protection devices won't be of any help. We'll all be done for.

Done for, done for, done for!

He slams his hand down on the table so hard that the beer mug tips over, its contents spilling onto the white oilcloth, flowing around the bread basket and dripping off the edge of the table. Christina goes to get the dishrag to wipe it up. She assures her father that the Führer will exhaust every possibility in order to peacefully resolve Germany's intolerable situation on its eastern border.

Everyone knows no eleven-year-old girl talks like that. That's how Nazi-Women's-League leader and Party member Rast talks.

Therefore—or at least so one might assume—it was for her, rather than for Christina, that the plate which suddenly struck the wall had been intended, as well as the jar of mustard, whose contents blossomed for a moment like a sunflower on the pale green wall. Christina, sitting in the target zone, had taken cover, and when she got up, her father was standing next to her. He seemed even taller than usual, his moleskin trousers hanging from his suspenders. A fly buzzed around the flypaper, then settled onto the sweet, sticky surface and tried to wrest itself free again.

A blue-checkered handkerchief wiped Christina's tears from her face. It smelled like sweat and a warm pants pocket. That was as much as her father could muster by way of asking her forgiveness, and a young girl in need of love must have figured out how to interpret such veiled signs of affection and learned to treasure them. She relished the moment, even after the handkerchief had long since disappeared back into its pocket. Some sort of explanation, no matter how inadequate, would have been welcome and might have eased the combination of guilt and self-pity that the young girl was feeling. But keeping quiet was what was called for. Her father left the kitchen without uttering a word, and without saying anything, her mother got up on a stool to wipe off the wall. Christina picked up the broken glass from the floor, then ran outside to join her friends in the chimney-sweep game. She chose her friend Gerda to be the wife, but she didn't choose anyone to be the baby, even though that sort of ruined the game. She was pretty stubborn about this decision. But when Gerda, giving in to peer pressure, pulled little Anneliese into the game—little Anneliese who with her club foot and crossed eyes would not have made any father or mother proud but who was happy to play her part, dragging her little right leg behind her—Christina had Kurt take over as the chimney sweep and defiantly stomped off. It was dangerous to change the rules of the game since you risked being considered a spoilsport, but this time, the spoilsport willingly assumed that risk. Maybe this was an attempt to give up her childish ways and find a way to connect with the world of grown-ups, where the rules seemed to be changing all the time.

During the night, Christina dreamed about a yellow flower. She climbed into it and lay sleeping in the petals that enveloped her and radiated the sweet smell of honey.

She was still sleeping when the war broke out. What must have awakened her were the conversations from the window that her mother was having with everybody who came past the house. On this particular morning, the beds stayed unmade, and the breakfast dishes remained in the sink. This tidy household, her mother's pride and joy, had sunk into a state of total neglect. But the war had actually started. It happened on a Friday, and school was called off.

By the time school started up again, the teacher had mounted next to the blackboard a map of the world on which the best pupil in geography, pointy-nosed Isolde, was permitted to track the advance of the German troops with multi-colored stickpins. The Blitzkrieg's stickpins marched over rivers and cities whose names were difficult to pronounce, until the German Army divisions met up with the Russians, at which point they stayed put in a line that stretched from East Prussia via Brest-Litovsk all the way to the Carpathian mountains.

Mars, the god of war, had either gone to sleep or was spending the winter somewhere else because of bad weather. That's the quiet before the storm, warned her father, who, like many previously imprisoned political activists, had spent the early days of the war detained under investigation. Ever since, for nights on end, he had been having secret meetings in his study with other activists, debating the issues, again risking his neck. Her mother let it be known that Herr Bohrer, the schoolteacher who lived opposite, was taking note of everybody who came and went from the Steiger house.

The school chorus is practicing songs about spring: *May has come and the flowers are in bloom, Only if your heart is heavy dare you stay at home.* Christina is not in the mood for singing, since she knows things are not good at home. Words overheard in the middle of the night: You're going to be the death of all of us! Get those pamphlets out of the house! At least think of your daughter!

The daughter stood at the top of the stairs. She would later have to admit that she slowly crept down the steps and hid crouching behind the hall door, thinking only of the warning "you're-going-to-be-the-death-of-us-all"—words that became a tangle of dark thoughts that dampened any sense of joy and obscured any ray of light.

Forgetfulness, lack of concentration, daydreaming—all these amounted to irresponsibility, according to Fräulein Rast, who had recently admonished Christina several times for not paying attention.

What is today's date? May 10th, a day of victory, especially for General Guderian and his Panzer Corps, who crossed the Maas near

Sedan. Isolde's index finger hesitates in the Argonne Forest and stops just outside Sedan. Fräulein Rast feels the need to stick the pin into the map herself, and since the location is an already well-known battlefield, she also recounts the slaughter that took place there during the last war.[11]

The term "slaughter" had definite associations for Christina, as it brought to mind the annual slaughter that took place at Oma Stina's, and which she and her cousin Erika always watched from the roof of the chicken coop. They stopped up their ears and tried to see who could keep watching the longest. Herr Zeh, the butcher, always wore a white apron that was splattered with blood from top to bottom.

War is also said to be bloody. From February to August 1916, German troops had carried out a very bloody offensive at Verdun. The slaughter at the Somme, on the other hand, was carried out by the Allies, supported by the vast industrial might of the United States. It was the heaviest bombardment of all time, lasting an entire week with hardly any let-up. The forward positions of the German forces were almost completely annihilated, but despite the destruction, they held on.

Under the command of Fräulein Rast, the pupils toured the slaughter sites, moving into the region around Arras, and then into Flanders, where they stopped along the Siegfried line until the bell rang for recess.

In the weeks that followed, the line of stickpins tracked the victorious troops, from Rotterdam south toward Amiens, from Arras on to Paris. Marianne Moser's father was killed, and Fräulein Rast thought it appropriate to observe a moment of silence: not to mourn

---

[11] The Meuse-Argonne Offensive, also known as the Maas-Argonne Offensive and the Battle of the Argonne Forest, was a major aspect of the final Allied offensive of World War I, lasting for more than a month and a half in September and November of 1918. It cost 28,000 German lives, 26,277 American lives, and an unknown number of French lives. (https://en.wikipedia.org/wiki/Meuse - Argonne_Offensive)

the fallen hero but rather to acknowledge the sacrifice that Marianne had made on behalf of the Führer. Because of her sacrifice, Marianne from now on would be the one permitted to add further stickpins—if, that is, there were any more to be added.

Anybody can look up the word *Krieg*, meaning "war," in the dictionary. It's a Germanic word, since the ancient Germans, who were experts in armed combat and had become militarily superior to all their neighbors, had had no need to borrow a term from another language. Terms like "air-raid protection," "bunker," "early warning," on the other hand, belong to the vocabulary of defense—words that are supposed to lessen the state of anxiety. A strategic air offensive is different from any previous kind of armed attack since it is uniquely capable of precisely targeting the heartland of the enemy in order to destroy it, just like the aerial attacks on London and Rotterdam. And since Christina lives in the heartland of one such enemy (already in April, British warplanes had begun bombing smaller German cities), she helps her father brick up the cellar windows. The cellar ceiling is shored up with iron beams, and provisions are piled up next to the pallets with their straw mattresses. Outside, arrows everywhere point the way to air raid shelters, and people have to practice finding their way down into them. Air Marshal Hermann Göring—who had solemnly promised the German people that not a single bomb would fall on German soil—can no longer be believed.

He lies like a rug, declares Tante Eva, as they harvest the new potatoes, all the while on the lookout in case an informer might be hiding in the neighboring furrow spying on them. *Medals, medals on his chest, so fat he cannot close his vest, in the Reichstag he is famed, Hermann, Hermann is his name!* Christina loves rhymes and is about to repeat this one, but BE CAREFUL! The enemy may be listening. Christina wants to know what an informer looks like. But she's told to be quiet.

The night before, the British supposedly had again dropped propaganda leaflets. But even worse, they were rumored to be dropping potato beetles. Because, as even the British know, without potatoes Germany cannot survive. Something has to be done. Extreme measures are called for. All school-aged children are drafted into their first action in the war and ordered to march single file through the rows of potatoes hunting for the beetles. The teachers have to investigate every sighting, including false alarms, and with the help of an enlarged photo, compare every unknown bug crawling around on the bushes with the beetle in the picture. To the great dismay of the pupils, the operation is soon called off, one reason being that no potato beetles are found, and another that the farmers are complaining about their trampled potato fields.

What had earlier simply been called English is now considered the language of the enemy. The enemy are the Eaton boys, whose faces in the English textbook have already been transformed into distorted grimaces by those in the class with artistic talent. Marianne has drawn a German tank in the middle of Trafalgar Square, while Trudel Harloff, whose father is a captain in the navy, has a German submarine cruising along the white cliffs of Dover. While London burns, Fräulein Rast drills them on the conjugation of the English verb "to do." Special bulletins report that London has been turned into a blast furnace with people on fire writhing in pain. Whereupon thousands more planes are dispatched over the English Channel on their mission of death.

Christina is terrified of fire. In German class she stutters while reciting a poem. The class snickers. The teacher gives Christina a questioning look and tries to fix her blond hairdo, a bun that despite her best efforts always seems to hang in a mess down her neck by the end of every class. Christina can't go on. Doris Lutz, known as the "Angel" because her curly red hair stands out around her freckled face as if charged with electricity, wants to take over. Fräulein Rast, however, who had no particular affection for such Renaissance angels and who had told Lotte, Doris's mother, numerous times that such a hair-do disqualified a young girl from participating in sports, calls on Marianne Moser instead: she is really good at sports, but gets stuck three times while reciting Goethe's *Erlkönig*.

An announcement from the principal's office: If there is an air-raid alarm during the night, the first two class periods the next morning will be cancelled. A preliminary air-raid alert signal does not count, since you are allowed to stay in bed for that. Reconnaissance planes only merit preliminary alert signals, and there were only reconnaissance flights until December 1940. But after that, it was the real thing! "Lights out!" is the command shouted from the street, and even though Christina's family always followed regulations and lowered their blackout shades every evening, they heed this order. Even a tiny ray of light might show through and be seen from the sky, and then….

Christina can't find her track suit in the dark. She should hurry up; searchlights are already scanning the sky. Christina is now hunting for her shoes. Flak can already be heard in the distance. Never mind your socks, come on, we don't want to be the last ones down.

Christina sits in the cellar and trembles. Mrs. Klein, who retreated into the stairwell even during lightning storms, keeps calling out hysterically for her husband, who's standing out in the courtyard smoking along with Christina's father. Smoking is not allowed in the cellar. Her father shuts the metal air-raid door behind him. If you can hear the bombs, the planes have already flown past. You hear the bombs, you feel the impact, the detonation. Plaster rains down from the cellar ceiling. Christina covers her ears, hears her own heart beating, and often holds her breath. A German girl must be brave, and tomorrow the first two periods at school will be cancelled. So, tomorrow no Latin and no Math. No small reward for a pupil who really hates Latin.

Herr Klein curses these damned Tommies. He's sitting on the pallet across from Christina and nervously rubs his chin with the back of his hand. If even the men are scared, it's going to be bad, and everybody knows that. She bites her fingernails and waits for the usual reprimand from her mother, but nothing is said. In an air-raid shelter the usual rules don't apply. In here there's nothing to do but wait and listen.

Up top it's gotten quiet and Herr Klein, mindful of his duty as air-raid warden, wants to go take a look. His wife, who is clinging tightly to him, won't let him go. It clearly bothers him not to be able to carry out his duty. Herr Nagel, who lodges with the Kleins, volunteers—due to both curiosity and a weak bladder—to step in for his landlord. He announces to everyone in the shelter that the city is on fire. Everyone streams out and heads to the embankment, which is high enough to afford a particularly good view of the city.

Weidenhof is on fire. No, that's farther toward the right; it's the center of town. There's a dispute about every geographical location. The village seems to have been spared. It's a moonlit night, and the children collect pieces of shrapnel that they trade with each other. Christina holds onto hers. Since it was a piece that had actually fallen into the Steiger's yard, she feels duty-bound to keep it. She will even take it with her to school the next morning.

The teacher describes the events of the previous night as a terrorist attack and promises the sixth graders that retribution will soon be forthcoming. Those British air pirates! All they do is bomb civilian homes and hospitals. They'll soon get theirs!

We'll fly over to England where the roses bloom so red,
we'll fly over to England and soon they'll all be dead.

Ingeborg is dead. She's not only dead, she has disappeared from the face of the earth, blown up by a high-explosive bomb, scattered to the four winds. They found only a crater out in the field where her house had once stood. "I can't believe it" was an all-too-common expression at the time. It was simply not possible to believe what was happening. Why this particular house, which stood several kilometers outside of town in the middle of a plum orchard behind the pumping station? The following afternoon half the village stood around the crater, amazed at its size, while Christina picked up the piano keys that were lying scattered around the field. For months she carried this treasure around in a cigar box. And from then on, she started skipping her piano lessons, since Ingeborg, her companion-in-misery—the one who always went in first and played her études for Fräulein Wetzel just as half-heartedly as Christina did—was no longer there.

Skipping piano lessons, just like skipping school, undermined the usual order of things. Nothing affects routine worse than questioning routine itself. How was one to carry on when nothing seemed to matter to anyone, when children could casually make their own decisions about what they wanted to do or not do? Her mother considered every infraction to be a violation of the natural order of things. Order has its place, even in wartime. We're not going to skip Christmas. On the contrary, at times when everything seems to be going off the rails, one needs to hold on to something that's a constant, the security that is found within one's family. And Christmas is, and always has been, a family celebration.

Tante Lisa, as usual, took charge. In this second year of the war she was especially well positioned to do so, since she had already moved her best things for safekeeping into the storage room of an inn in the Odenwald, and thus had plenty of space in her living room for all the guests. The big dining room table had disappeared; in its place was the old table from the garden covered with a damask tablecloth. On the walls you could see the dark outlines where the "masterpieces" that the family had made fun of had hung; for instance, the still-life, a basket of fruit that she had bought for a ridiculously low price from a Jewish family about to emigrate. The Dahms, who had had to leave abruptly, had in fact wanted to give it to her, but she said she had refused.

Where the Biedermeier corner cabinet had stood, there was now a small space heater, since there was no longer enough coke for central heating. People had begun to live provisionally because the future appeared to offer nothing but one wrenching change after another. Nonetheless, Lisa pulled out all the stops. There was roast goose and homemade noodles, and Onkel Werner, generous as always, contributed his last bottles of Bordeaux. In his toast, he expressed his heartfelt hope that peace would come soon. At the children's table in the kitchen, however, a battle was underway because Ernst August, who always had to play the big shot at home, had taken charge of doling out the Christmas cookies. Despite knowing that Christina was especially fond of the little anise cookies, he had put just a single gingerbread man and a few spritz cookies on her plate. Christina was not going to let him get away with such an injustice and made a big fuss. But calling her own cousin a stupid nitwit, even if he was known to be the family lunkhead, went too far. She should take it back! But how can one recant when one firmly believes what has been said? She had only insisted on what was right, and instead, she should now be sorry for causing this argument, since in the meantime Tante Lisa and Tante Käthe were arguing because Tante Käthe had come to the defense of her sweet little Christina. Christina would never forget that, nor the two little anise cookies that her favorite aunt had placed on her plate, and she would always stick up for her Tante Käthe, even if the rest of the family wanted to wring her aunt's neck.

Tante Klara kept on teasing her brothers-in-law and her brother Peter, whom she was trying to drink under the table—something she would not succeed at. Onkel Peter, who was already on his way to becoming an alcoholic, could hold more liquor than the rest of them put together. Oma Stina could have gone on at length about that but held her tongue, since everybody around the table had heard it a million times. Tante Rosa, the first war widow of her generation, was seated in the place of honor at the end of the table, staring blankly at the rest of them. She was in mourning over her Robert, who had fought in the battle of Narvik, and didn't notice the knowing looks that her sisters were exchanging about Klara, their youngest sister, who was cut from different cloth: a real beauty, tall and slender with jet-black hair parted down the middle and drawn back tightly into a bun. As the last child born in the last days of the last war, she had always been her mother's problem child. She should rot in hell! This would be Oma Stina's blasphemous pronouncement when she later learned that Klara had gotten herself pregnant by, of all people, a Polish forced laborer she'd been working with at Herr David's farm, helping to bring the crop in. Klara would never admit to it, but her husband, who was now standing watch for the Fatherland at the Russian front, would be able to count on his fingers and figure out that he could not be the child's father.

A Polish whore in other words, and if that gets out, she'll land in jail. It has to be kept secret, so the family council plans to send her away for a while to a farmstead near Lake Constance. But Klara, irresponsible as always, decides to take the risk and gives birth in Oma Stina's sugar-beet field. Oma Stina drives her home, lying on a sack of beets in the cart, past Herr David's farmhouse, where it was said the Polish laborer stood at the gate and wept.

Later, once Christina had pieced together the tidbits of information that she had garnered from various overheard whisperings, it seemed there were several versions of this story, but no one could provide concrete evidence as to which one was true. In any case, the Pole returned after the war to look up Klara, but she apparently turned him away at the door. Thus, he never got to see his daughter, who was living somewhere in the Rhineland and was, as Tante Klara regretfully admitted, cut from different cloth.

The truth is, Christina had visited Tante Klara when she was laid up for several weeks with childbed fever. She had brought her a bottle of red wine and a few fresh eggs that she thought might help her aunt feel better. And during this visit, Christina confided to Tante Klara that she had not been able to bring herself to kiss Oma Stina because she kept hearing those awful words her grandmother had uttered to the family members sworn to secrecy. It was unimaginable that a mother could wish her child dead. But her grandmother could not be held responsible for Christina's subsequent nightmares, dreams in which her own mother waited until the very last minute to save her from some awful fate. Those were the nightmares of many children during the war, afraid of being abandoned in a world in which nothing was secure, condemned to wait anxiously for whatever would come next.

In the spring of 1941, it was almost like peace time—at least it seemed that way— although the number of different battlefronts was increasing. Theaters of war, they were called, and Christina imagined this term—theater-of-war—as being a huge auditorium, like the fancy movie theater in the city where from your private box or a seat in the balcony you could take part in the battles. Just like the battles Ernst August waged with his tin-soldiers, battles she always had to

participate in when the women got together for an afternoon of nee-
dlework. They were sitting in Tante Lisa's sunroom crocheting—and
knitting together the latest bits of news.

Christina's not playing fair, the resident son complained, barging
in on the ladies who, at the moment, were busy gossiping about the
delicate matter of Frau Wolf's lover. But her husband pampers her
like a baby, Christina overheard them say, since she had followed
right on the heels of her accuser and stood listening in the doorway.
In her wildest imagination, Christina couldn't see how scrawny Herr
Wolf could possibly baby his quite corpulent wife. Christina's not
following the rules. They're my soldiers!

Possession being nine-tenths of the law, the scales of justice were
weighted in Ernst August's favor. Christina was told to please follow
the rules that had been made by the soldiers' owner. Enough! That's
it! Scram, both of you!

It should be made clear here that Christina was not really being
unfair. She just wanted, for once, to be the one to command the Prus-
sians in the battle of Rossbach. Ernst August, as usual, had put her
in charge of the French, but she had refused to pull back her infantry
and instead seized the opportunity to attack the Prussian cavalry on
its flank. True, that was not how it had happened back in 1757. But
Christina couldn't have cared less—just this one time she wanted
to win.

Truth be known, Christina was never unfair. She always divided
things equally. For example, the single piece of pastry left over from
the kaffeeklatsch. Born with an innate sense of precision, she cut it
into two pieces and, confident that they were exactly the same size,
let Ernst August have his pick. But the master of the tin soldiers, pretending to be generous, said she could have them both. Christina
would have liked to exercise self-control over her love of puff pastry
and refuse to eat any of it, but figured she'd leave that sort of self-

denial to the cousin who, despite the food shortage, could wolf down a whole tin of Bahlsen cookies in one sitting. We have connections, he would brag, every time she caught him eating treats.

For her birthday, Christina wished that, in addition to a new photo album, she, too, could have "connections." What she got instead was a collectible porcelain teacup, a standard item for the hope chests of girls who would never manage to acquire a complete set of china. Ach, her mother sighed, a sigh that was becoming louder and more and more frequent now that they were already having to use some of the bed linens that had been intended for Christina's trousseau, the set trimmed in bobbin lace.

Christina let her mother know that she needn't worry about that, since she had no intention of getting married. She wanted to be an architect and carry on her father's business, so she wouldn't need a husband, nor bed linens with bobbin lace or any other such stuff.

Very funny, that's a good one!

Just you wait; when you're older, you'll feel differently about that. Allusions like this had lately been made by her cousin Tilde, who was three years older and whose mother, Susanne, Oma Stina's second eldest, had married a man from Cologne who worked as a boatman on the Rhein and lived on his boat. So that Tilde could attend trade school, she had been sent to board with Oma Stina. Tilde frequently stopped by to visit her Tante Elise, trying to charm her way into the household, since she didn't like it at Oma Stina's. There she had to take care of the goats and the chickens, and besides that, her grandmother always plaited Tilde's curly red hair into braids, since Oma Stina was convinced that nobody could think or work with hair hanging in their face. Tilde looked just like the angel blowing the trumpet that was carved on the console of the church organ. She had the same chubby cheeks and curvaceous rear end that moved rhythmically side to side as she sauntered down the street. This exciting sight caused a significant increase in the heart rates of the village's young men, especially Edgar Wagner's. And indeed, before long, Tilde became involved with him. The two of them would meet secretly on the canal embankment, and once, Christina and Gerda followed them and watched from their hiding place as Edgar and Tilde kissed. Gerda thought it was fascinating, but for Christina, it was suddenly just embarrassing. She breathed more easily when the couple lay down in the meadow by the dam, and the grass hid them from view.

Humans ripen, just like cherries and the fruit on the espaliered trees. It would be great if that were all there was to it. But any time her mother made an attempt to broach the subject of the facts of life, Christina played dumb, affecting such a look of innocence that her mother just let the subject drop.

In biology class, the topic was ferns and how they demonstrated a generational alternation between sexual and asexual reproduction. Frau Schneider, PhD, passed around a fern leaf that showed the spores of the first stage developing on the underside. However, once again no connection was made between this and human reproduction. As usual, there were only intimations that something was about to happen.

It was already happening to some of the girls in the class, who were sometimes allowed to sit on the bench during gym class and watch while the others toiled away on the parallel bars or tried to improve upon their mounts and lifts on the pommel horse to satisfy the teacher. It was a matter of steeling your body, and the bruises that you got along the way were signs that you had given it your best effort. Christina's legs showed how hard she had worked. Her mother was convinced that she had suffered permanent damage. Twice Christina had fallen off the bars and put a gash in her right knee, which now refused to heal. Sister Martha, the rough, gruff Protestant nurse who was responsible for treating minor injuries, always mercilessly ripped off the bloody, pus-filled bandage and then, without a shred of sympathy, painted iodine on the wound as if she were on a mission to punish girls who hadn't been baptized. Christina therefore sought out Sister Fakunda instead, the Catholic nurse who slowly removed the bandage with her cool white hands and didn't miss the opportunity to bring up God, and also Jesus, who hung crucified on the wall and watched over children who constantly gashed open their knees. She even stopped by one evening to talk to Christina's parents about saving their child's soul, if that might still be possible? It was not possible. Christina was, and would remain, unbaptized.

Being an atheist did have certain advantages. For example, you didn't need to attend religion class at school, which meant that three days a week you could stay in bed an hour longer or hang out with the other heathen children—if you could figure out who they were. At first, Christina was the only one, so she usually sat in the schoolyard or chatted with the janitor until the Protestant chaplain and the Catholic deacon came out, bade each other a friendly farewell, and hurried off to their respective houses of worship without taking any notice of the young heathen. She would have liked to know what went on in religion class but didn't dare ask. All the catechism booklets had long since been put away by the time she came into the classroom, and her classmates acted as if nothing special had taken place during the preceding period. But many of them later renounced the church, since the Führer did not like taking a back seat to Jesus. They claimed they still believed in God but stood around the schoolyard complaining about the others, particularly the Catholics who went to confession on Saturdays instead of showing up for meetings.

Which is actually more important: going to confession or doing your duty? Christina, of course, thought duty was, since confession had always seemed to her to be something odd, almost unnatural.

Once, Trudy Wagner had shown Christina her list of things to confess—which was in itself a sin that Trudy had to add to the list of all the other sins she had committed during the first weeks of her close friendship with Christina. On the list, Trudy had confessed to being unchaste but was certain that God would forgive this sin. After looking the word up in the dictionary, Christina couldn't imagine, no matter how hard she tried, how Trudy could have done something promiscuous without Christina having noticed. In any case, Christina was opposed to confession and thus joined those who claimed to be "believers," though at school she did not change her designation as an atheist. The "believers" didn't pray; they put their faith in the Führer.

In wartime, everyone learns how to pray. That was one of Oma Stina's favorite sayings, and indeed, she was praying more frequently these days since, despite the cataract in her right eye, she could clearly see where things were headed. They couldn't take her son from her anymore, since already, back in the summer of '41, drunken Peter had cracked his head open when he had ridden his motorcycle into the rear end of a truck. But she had five sons-in-law, none of whom were exempt from military service. As each one was called up, she'd put their photograph behind the glass door of her kitchen cabinet. She had always tried not to favor any one of her sons-in-law over the other. When they came to say goodbye, she gave each a care package with a loaf of homemade rye bread and a chunk of sausage or ham. If they didn't return, she had the photo framed and hung it in her parlor next to the crepe-bedecked picture of her late husband. On the chest of drawers there was a picture of little Marie, her second youngest, who had lived for years in an institution because she was not right in the head. She had died suddenly and unexpectedly just a week after Peter. Another clear sign that bad luck always has company. Oma Stina supposedly often sat in her parlor and grieved. But she never cried. Her once sharp eyes just became duller with each loss. Her thoughts began to dwell in the past, since the present, which was tearing her world apart, had become impossible to understand.

Instead of going into the bunker when there was an air raid alarm, she'd wander off into the fields. When the all-clear had sounded, they'd often find her far beyond the village limits, resting on a satchel containing her good black woolen dress, her patent-leather shoes, and her hymnal. She had made it very clear to her daughters that she did not want to be buried in a shroud.

And she was indeed laid out in her good black dress, only a week before an aerial mine would blow her little house to smithereens. It was obvious that the British still couldn't aim accurately, since they certainly wouldn't have intended to bomb Oma Stina's house. The family was grateful that God in His mercy had spared her this misfortune. Those who had not been spared stood around looking at the gaping crater surrounded by the remnants of the cellar walls, searching for whatever might be left.

But they were looking in the wrong place. Two streets over, at the end of the Pfarrgasse to be specific, Frau Zimmer, while tilling her garden in spring, would unearth a leather case. Inside was a Bible that had been there all winter, somewhat protected by its case from the wind and weather. The Bible had been dedicated to the bride and groom, Peter and Christina Berry, whose descendants naturally launched a search for anything else that might be found in Frau Zimmer's yard. Even the neighboring yards were not off limits, and after a while, there was a pile of little treasures that had been retrieved from the damp spring earth where some weeds were already growing and in which the earthworms had already begun doing the work necessary to prepare for the upcoming planting season.

If you think earthworms are disgusting, you have to make yourself useful in some other way. Christina therefore collected all the objects that had been found and put labels on them. A row of dented pot lids, milk cans, cups with missing handles, and silver-plated flatware graced Frau Zimmer's garden wall. Oma Stina, whose household effects consisted of an eclectic collection of hand-me-downs from her better-off daughters, would have been pleased that these same daughters would later be gathering up all this old stuff and taking it back to where it had come from. She would also have approved of the fact that the bombed-out ruins of her house ended up being deeded over to her youngest daughter (Klara), who would live in the animals' quarters, covered with only a makeshift roof, until the end of the war.

Klara had a wall built to separate her living space from the goats'. She whitewashed it and laid down a floor made from old boards. Around the bed that she shared with Little Tina hung a blue-and-white checkered curtain. It's just temporary, Klara kept saying, and when it's all over, I'll tear everything down and have the place rebuilt. She planned to add another story with a little balcony over the garden, and with this in mind, she had already begun collecting bricks that she piled up in the back yard. She herself drew up the plans for her little house and hung them over the corner bench that she had cobbled together so that she could always have the plans in view when she was sitting at the table knitting or mending and thinking about the future. No matter how near or far the goal, as long as one keeps it in sight, one can keep moving in that direction, and Tante Klara's hopes and dreams grew in proportion to her pile of bricks.

There were people who still knew what they were hoping for. For them, their hopes hinged on the word "end." Some of them still believed that the war might end in the ultimate victory despite the decision in June of '41 to invade Russia, and the Soviet resistance obviously was not letting up. Others preferred even a terrible end to unending terror. Christina's mother belonged to this group. Her father, on the other hand, introduced terror to the family long before the end. Namely, he had once again been summoned to City Hall. At a card game, he had purportedly made a comment that was judged to be treasonous. For the protection of both the State and the People, a stricter interpretation of the ordinance prohibiting what was termed "verbal propaganda" had recently been implemented. Under the new rules, it now had to be determined whether the offender had intended to influence another person or persons to take action against the State.

People were said to have gathered outside City Hall, wanting to find out if in fact Philipp would keep his word, namely, that he'd bite off his tongue rather than ever utter the "Heil Hitler" greeting.

It was reported that he had indeed simply said "Guten Morgen"—which gave like-minded people something to mull over without having to risk anything themselves. As it turned out, his accuser failed to appear for the proceedings, so Christina's father had gotten off with only a strongly worded warning from the investigating committee.

Why can't he simply keep his mouth shut? Why can't he just let it be? There really isn't anything he can change. You can't swim against the current. There's plenty of evidence for that. Hadn't they already forbidden him to practice as an architect back in '38 when they denied his request to cancel his membership in the Reich Chamber of the Arts? That must have been grist for the mill of his colleague, the architect and Party member Kleinhans, whose signature was thereafter required on all of Philipp's blueprints before they could be submitted for approval. Somewhere along the way you should have tried to make your peace with them, Elise told Philipp, then you'd be exempt from the military, just like Kleinhans is.

Christina's mother, who once again was having a heart-to-heart talk with Tante Lisa, acted as though she could predict the future. She is convinced that when this is all over, nobody will give a damn who belonged to which organization. And while she will ultimately end up being right about this, for now she is up against the unassailable resistance of her husband, who will never give an inch when it's a matter of principle. To hell with him, to put it bluntly.

And while she's at it, Christina's mother digs out of the drawer the receipt for the radio that had the following notice printed on the back: *Those who listen to prohibited radio stations are enemies of the state. In October, fifty-six-year old Louis Birch was sentenced to death by the People's Supreme Court. Ever since the beginning of the war, he spread the inflammatory propaganda of the enemy. By means of this abominable behavior, he stabbed our fighting forces in the back and thus relinquished his right to remain a member of society.*

So, whatever you hear on the Sachsenwerk radio tuned to short-wave frequency, you keep to yourself. You don't even tell your own sister that her son, declared missing months ago, is being held by the British as a prisoner of war. Everybody knows that his submarine had been sunk off the coast of Gibraltar. But only those who listen to illegal shortwave radio broadcasts know that the British had fished the entire crew out of the Mediterranean. They even know the names of the men who were rescued, but they can't pass on such information. You can only look on in silence as Tante Anna seems to age years in just a matter of weeks. All you can do is feign sympathy until she finally gets word from the Red Cross that her eldest son is still alive.

From then on, Christina will withdraw every evening when preparations for engaging in this treasonous activity are underway. She is not interested in hearing that the Germans have not yet succeeded in breaking through the defensive line encircling Moscow and that it already starts snowing there in October. It would doubtless upset her to learn that the British still have ample reserves of airplanes and air crews at their disposal.

Dr. Link, the new math teacher who had served on the front lines, claims that the supply of British aircraft is being supplemented by planes sent over by the Americans. With the chalk clenched in his prosthetic hook, he scribbles on the blackboard equations with two unknowns that Isolde, as usual without even being called upon, proceeds to solve as quickly as an adding machine. Her hair, gathered behind her neck like Schiller's and tied with black ribbon ever since her brother's heroic death, bobs rhythmically from one equation to the next. Doris Lutz, whose average grade in math is a D-minus, makes a face at her. The class starts to giggle and Isolde, from whom no one would have expected such theatrics, begins to shout: Don't you realize my brother is dead! The class looks on in disbelief as she tries to pull the mourning ribbon out of her hair and collapses in front of the podium, a bundle of misery.

Isolde never returned to school. They must have informed her at the sanatorium in the Black Forest that the school was no longer standing. After the last bombing attack, a large part of the inner city lay in ruins, and most of the schoolgirls were sent away to a boarding school outside the city.

Christina's father considered the boarding school to be nothing but a Hitler Youth camp and wouldn't let his daughter go. With great difficulty he managed to get her enrolled in a high school for boys in a neighboring town. He confided to the director, who had initially refused to accept her into a boys school, that he had already received his orders to report for duty, and in his absence, his daughter needed to look after her ailing mother.

It was true that her father would soon be called up, but Christina had a hard time looking him in the eye when he mentioned an "ailing mother," since it was the first time she had ever caught him in a lie.

Only many years later would she come to understand that this lie had been his last desperate attempt to keep his child from falling under the influence of the state-sanctioned sorcerers.

Those who are left behind are duty bound to write letters to the soldiers in the family. You're supposed to do everything possible to keep them connected to home, but you are not supposed to burden them with bad news. Thus, you can't tell your father that your mother has hurt her back while helping to build the air-raid shelter and for weeks has not been able to climb stairs but nonetheless continues to lug concrete blocks, since anyone who doesn't contribute to the work will not be let into the underground sanctuary next time. Even if her very own husband was the man who had drawn up the plans and persuaded the Catholic priest to let the empty space next to the Brother Konrad Chapel be used for this purpose. According to her father's technical calculations, the bunker should withstand the bombing, although it probably couldn't survive a direct hit. But what's the likelihood of the enemy aiming a bomb to land directly on this tiny speck of a place within the entire German Reich? The odds seem to favor the people who live on Hindenburgstrasse, and so, with these probabilities in mind, they are motivated to keep going, carrying tubs of mortar well into the night.

On his last leave before being sent to the Eastern Front, Christina's father helps install the iron entrance door and dedicate the bunker. Frau Klein donates a case of beer for the occasion, and Christina plays the new concertina that she has inherited from her cousin Kurt, who was killed on the Russian front. She plays: *We are all comrades, at the front and home as well*, the only song she knows how to play, since Tante Eva had given her the instrument only a few weeks ago. Tante Eva felt that giving away Kurt's things any sooner would have been like desecrating his grave, even though she doesn't know whether Kurt actually has a grave in Russia. As a favor to Tante Eva, Christina learns the song about the soldier on the bank of the Volga, standing watch for the Fatherland. When Christina finally can play it for her after lots of practicing, she hears her aunt sobbing at the kitchen sink where she has just taken two cups from the pile of dirty dishes and rinsed them. With her apron, she dries both the cups and her tears. One of the cups, the one with the crack that runs between "silver" and "anniversary," she places in front of Christina. It's a cup of peppermint tea, Tante Eva's cure-all. Kurt had always loved to drink peppermint tea and Kurt had been such a good boy and he had sacrificed to save up the money for the concertina and so Christina should be careful with it and always keep it in its case so that the bellows don't dry out . . . .

Tante Eva's legs are swollen again. Christina brings over a stool and helps her aunt put her legs up. How can I possibly stand in line for hours on legs like these only to find that there's hardly anything in the stores to buy? They're buying everything up on the black market, those scoundrels! By scoundrels, Tante Eva presumably means the people who are better off, who, because of their connections or their deeper pockets, can buy things to supplement their rations, creating shortages for everybody else. Herr Seitz, the grocer, was one of those people with "Vitamin C," that is, "connections." Suddenly one day, his wife appeared in a new silver fox coat. They've got their sources, but that just makes it harder and harder for us to buy bread. Christina decides that if such an otherwise good-natured soul as Tante Eva is acting like this, it must be because she's hungry, so she takes it upon herself to help out her aunt.

When there's not enough to eat, all sorts of hostility creeps into people's personal relationships, hostility of a primitive nature. Even the bonds that hold together that basic community—one's extended family—can be ruptured. Tante Anna had illegally butchered a pig but hadn't shared the bounty with the others. Instead, she had traded a smoked ham for a hundred pounds of potatoes. She's living high on the hog while we're practically starving! In order to keep the peace, Tante Eva reluctantly decides to slaughter her twelve-year-old brood goose and barters it for Russian sunflower oil. She gives Elise a liter of it. But there still are no potatoes to cook in it.

Christina knows where there are potatoes. She has watched farmer Joachim bury half of his harvest in a sand pit, and she's marked the location with a rock. Under cover of darkness, she sneaks out to the field. As soon as the field guard with his German shepherd dog has crossed over the canal bridge and she knows that the coast will be clear for a little while, she starts digging. When she finishes digging—let's be honest and call it stealing—she sits down under the canal bridge with her sack of potatoes and laughs so hard it brings tears to her eyes. Maybe she actually did cry, not because she felt guilty, but because she was deathly afraid of German shepherds.

The next day, roasted potatoes once again appeared on Tante Eva's table, and Elise made boiled potatoes with herring. Tante Eva couldn't decide whether or not stealing food was really a sin. At home, not a word was ever said about where these wonderful potatoes had come from. Christina was disappointed in her mother for not saying anything, as she really wanted a co-conspirator in this illegal appropriation of someone else's property. But soon after, it turned out that her friend Gerda was a perfect candidate for this role. The only problem was that Gerda always started giggling when things got dicey, with the unfortunate result that they often peed their pants.

How often those two girls came home with their underpants wet, dragging a sack of sugar beets or cabbage behind them. The farmers, who would have much preferred to barter their produce for a Persian rug or a set of Rosenthal china, complained to their field guards that they were not doing their jobs. So they brought in more dogs, and stealing food got more and more dangerous every night.

Being hungry. Having hunger pangs, that gnawing feeling in your belly. Dreaming of chocolate. The younger children had it easier since, for example, they had no idea what a *Mohrenkopf* was. It was only the older kids whose mouths watered when Christina went on and on about this chocolate covered marshmallow confection that you used to be able to buy from the stands at the various church festivals back in the days when everything could still be had. These days you have to go trudging through the fields of stubble, your legs and feet wrapped in rags, gleaning whatever left-behind stalks of grain you find and taking them to the mill where, if you're lucky and the miller is in a good mood, you can maybe get two pounds of flour for the whole day's work.

The flour was first made into bread, then the bread was used for bread soup, the last of which ended up getting moldy because you never got a chance to eat it, since every enemy squadron headed towards southern Germany seemed to fly over their part of the country—the S-R quadrants.[12] Instead of concert music in response to listener requests, all you heard on the radio these days was *Flakfunk*—the broadcast of information about enemy air sorties— so you could follow the paths of the bombers. If they hadn't turned away by quadrant S-R-1, Christina would leave the table with her soup uneaten—such things could ruin one's appetite. Once, in the middle of the night when everyone was asleep, she sneaked back into the house from the bunker because she was hungry. As she sat in the dark spooning up the abandoned soup, she suddenly realized that it tasted moldy. After that she went several days without eating a thing, and

---

[12] The area of the air-defense grid monitored by Saarland Radio.

Elise couldn't do anything as her daughter, who was skinny to begin with, got even skinnier.

We should just leave everything behind, go to Tante Lisa's in the Odenwald, and wait there for this all to be over with. Better to go and work yourself to the bone with the farmers than with the recently announced Women's Work Corps for Defense of the Reich. Or, if you couldn't escape to the Odenwald, maybe you could escape by getting sick. Despite having been put on notice by the district medical authorities because of unwarranted medical diagnoses that might enable the local population to circumvent the newly promulgated labor requirements, Dr. Hoffmann declared Elise Steiger unable to work due to an inflammation of the heart muscle. The mothers of Christina's classmates, who for the most part belonged to the elite, showed up voluntarily at designated Party work sites in order the avoid being ordered to join a labor brigade. Who would really want to work in an armament factory like, for example, Lenni Hartmann, who once, during the movie's weekly newsreel about the war effort on the home front, had whispered to Christina that it was a lot different at the factory where she worked.

Lenni, orphaned as a small child, had been sent by her relatives to work in a factory at the tender age of fifteen. As a result, before the war the only people she got to know were men, and therefore she lost her "feminine nature"—as it was always called—and in the end, also lost her reputation. Having to sit next to Lenni is the penalty you pay if you come late to the movie theater, where currently they are showing the film *Vienna Blood*. Next to Lenni there's always an empty seat, since she can't help but keep up a running commentary, verbalizing what is happening on the screen, so that those sitting in the rows behind and in front of her have to frequently ask her to be quiet.

The images of Field Marshall Rommel evoke a few cheers. The scenes from the Eastern Front mainly show the defeat of the enemy as planned. Lenni calls it a retreat which, according to her sources—she knows some soldiers on leave from the front—is not going according to plan. But the last image on the newsreel shows a Soviet plane being shot down, and Lenni thinks that's just terrific.

In the middle of a Viennese waltz, the lights go out. AIR-RAID WARNING!

Lenni takes Christina's hand and forcibly pulls her away from the emergency exit. We'll never get out that way. You'll be trampled to death.

Lenni tears down the blackout curtain from one of the windows, knocks out the pane with a chair, shoves Christina up onto it, and pushes her through the broken window. Outside, you can see the bright light from where the first targeting bombs were dropped. The engine sounds grow louder and louder, signaling the imminent attack. Knowing there's not enough time to get to a bunker, Christina stands petrified in the doorway of a building. The stairwell is already full of people seeking shelter. Lenni supposedly found her cowering on the ground and, without saying a word, dragged her into a cellar. What Christina remembered was the smell of machine oil in Lenni's canvas jacket and hair, and Lenni's hands—calloused from years of operating a milling machine—which Christina held onto for dear life. But she left it up to Lenni, who from then on was frequently an uninvited guest at the Steigers, to relate the details of the whole experience. I'm telling you, Frau Steiger, God only knows what would have happened if I hadn't been there, she insisted.

It was Lenni who brought a laborer from the East to Christina's mother because the poor girl desperately needed a bath. Otherwise, she'd get scabies. In the barracks that had been quickly erected next to the factory to house the forced laborers, there was no running water, and in Lenni's little attic room over the store, there naturally wasn't any either. Lenni herself went to the public baths every week.

The Russian girl was named Anna. She couldn't speak German, but with a few Russian phrases and a lot of hand gestures, Lenni kept the conversation going.

She's a White Russian, captured, parents dead, two brothers, both soldiers.

Anna kept her hand over her mouth, probably to hide the wide gap from missing teeth. She giggled, embarrassed, when they asked her how old she was. She raised both hands once, then a single hand—that would be fifteen—then three fingers, just three. Lenni leaned toward Anna and with a smile pulled off her kerchief, exposing her head, shaved almost completely bald above her broad forehead. Lice, explained Lenni, hoping to calm Christina's alarmed look.

Anna understood and pulled a photo out of the little sack she was holding between her knees. Anna leaning against a garden fence, hair down to her shoulders, a perfect smile. Anna at home. Christina's mother reached into the fruit basket for an apple, polished it with her apron, and put it on the table in front of Anna, who nodded and stuffed it into her bag. Christina went and got her concertina and played for Anna the song about the soldier on the bank of the Volga. Lenni clapped in approval, but Anna did not. She made sounds like a deaf mute, which she pushed out from her lips with her outstretched hands. Lenni tried to put into words what was going on.

She's so homesick; she's dying of homesickness.

Christina's father in Russia is also homesick. You can read it between the lines. Tante Anna's Karl, writing from his POW camp in Canada, says that the countryside around Ottawa reminds him of home. He is also learning English. Christina is struggling with her Latin. And with Physics and Chemistry. Her male classmates are far more advanced than she is, especially in the natural sciences. Catching up to them seemed out of the question until the older pupils got drafted into air-defense service and the daily assignments had to be shortened, since those serving in the anti-aircraft installations had little time to study. One person's misfortune is another's good luck.

The unlucky ones who had been called into service were visited during the week by teachers who held classes in the barracks. On weekends, classmates would come to see them and admire the guns covered with camouflage netting and look around the radio control center.

Germany cannot be defeated from the air—this according to the junior officer who placed the headphones on Christina so she could listen to the anti-aircraft channel: At present there are no enemy squadrons in German air space.

And when the squadrons do come, you are glad to be at home sitting in a bunker and not stationed on the southern outskirts of town where your classmates are busy playing "total war."

"Total war" is a German invention. In such a war, there are no victors and no vanquished—only those who survive and those who do not—this according to the Führer in his Proclamation to the German People. On the eastern front, cities were being cleared out without any resistance, or else recaptured. Christina's father was only involved in clearing places out. A soldier on leave from the front brought them a letter from him. Under the circumstances, he was doing all right. And he was right. It could have been a lot worse. Fourteen people associated with the Worker's Movement, among them her father's old comrade Hans Kupka, were sentenced to death by the Second Criminal Commission of the People's Court. They were indicted for having participated in the production and distribution of the anti-fascist newspaper *The Harbinger*. It was determined that by their actions they had tried to hinder and compromise the will of the German People to take up arms in self-defense.

The bright red placards on the advertising kiosks announced that the accused had been sentenced to death by guillotine. An informer had penetrated this group of resistance fighters and betrayed them. Ever since the group's imprisonment, many of their comrades had been in grave danger. They were on the run, and you'd be putting your own life in danger if you attempted to help them.

Her mother started to bolt the doors and windows at night before she turned out the lights. She held her breath whenever she came into Christina's room. But Christina slept soundly and didn't notice when, in the middle of the night, someone started pounding on the door at the landing. It was the whispering that awoke her. Quiet negotiations were taking place in the hallway. The ring holding the house keys was taken off its hook, and then a shadow scurried past the crack under her bedroom door.

Even if she had noticed the next morning that the key to the construction shed was missing, Christina wouldn't have let on. It was only when she came home from school and wanted to feed her rabbits, and her mother pretended to be surprised that she couldn't find the key, that Christina smelled trouble. No, that's going too far. No, you can't do this to me! Her mother, caught red-handed, could only promise her daughter that she would be able to feed the rabbits the next day. So, tomorrow he'll be gone? She, her mother said, she. It was the woman with whom, on New Year's Eve of 1934–35, Elise had distributed leaflets in deserted streets and dark doorways, in public phone booths and private mailboxes. They had also launched flyers into the air using a small mortar. But it hadn't done any good. And these days, it would do even less. Christina wanted her mother to agree with her, wanted her reassurance that resistance was futile, and thus her promise that Christina would not suffer the same fate as the Kupka daughters.

At the evening meeting of the Young Girls League, they sang *No more beautiful country in our time, than the one right here we find.* By this time Christina had in fact become the section leader and had managed to acquire the full uniform, so it fell to her to mark the younger daughter of the executed Herr Kupka as "not present." Titti, the group leader, knew enough to control her indignation about the high treason committed by the father of one of her very own girls. Her usual high ringing voice took on a deep somber tone appropriate to the seriousness of the situation. She reminded the Young Leaguers of their duty to be true to the Fatherland, because *Germany, you must stand as our light, even if we lose the fight.*

It was only on the way home, when she was riding her bicycle past the construction shed, that Christina had serious thoughts about the idea of "losing the fight." In there, she supposed, the woman on the run had probably crept beneath the floorboards to hide out for the night. She should have felt sorry for this poor woman whose life was in mortal danger, but she couldn't muster such compassion. She was only upset when she admitted to herself that all she wanted was for this woman, this stranger, to be gone, far, far away.

It was impossible to go to sleep. Her fears only worsened when she imagined the mechanically operated blade of the guillotine crashing down. From then on, it was Christina who bolted the doors and windows. How could her mother have been so blind as to not notice that her daughter panicked every time the doorbell rang, constantly parted the curtains to look out at the street from which misfortune would come if it came? No, when it came.

It didn't come. Instead, one night a man came. His head tilted, wearing a peaked cap pulled down low on his forehead, he suddenly appeared at the kitchen window. He wanted to know if they were alone. As if she had been called by name, Christina got up and opened the front door for him. Without taking off his cap, he went straight down the hall into the kitchen and shut the door behind him. Christina sat on the steps with her head on her knees and stuck her fingers in her ears. She was so afraid she wanted to cry but choked back her sobs. She started to hum a song. The man didn't stay long, and when he left, he gave her a quick, rather furtive wave of his hand, signaling to Christina that from now on she belonged to those in the know.

She should have been told that those in the know could only be arrested if their participation could be proven. Instead, she was only told that she could again feed the rabbits in the morning.

There's no school today!

Christina slowly unwound herself from the down comforter and stared at the lighted rectangle that framed her mother's silhouette.

Today there's no school.

In the morning, her mother was inclined to repeat herself, since nothing she said seemed to register with her daughter. Christina was definitely not an early bird, so even a wake-up call as welcome as this one didn't make her want to get out of bed. She pulled the covers up over her head while her mother felt her way across the room to raise the blackout shade. As usual, she stumbled over the rucksack that was strategically placed so that Christina could quickly grab it and take it into the bunker at the first sound of an air-raid alarm.

At the moment, the treasures it contained included her book of poems, an album containing her collection of movie star cards, a blue envelope with photos, and letters from the front sent by cousins and friends who, during lulls in the action, took the time to write home. Since she switched up the contents of her rucksack almost every week, Christina could imagine that in the end she'd be able to rescue everything that was near and dear to her. Her mother let the shade snap up to the top and opened the window, a firm believer in the benefits of fresh air. Christina should hurry up, as she needed to be at the staging point in front of City Hall in half an hour.

It was Friday. You could smell it. Her mother was polishing the floor, and while she was at it, she relayed to her daughter, who was sitting there eating her bread and jam, the latest news that had been circulating from window to window since early morning. The inner city was still in flames, even though fire brigades from all over the area had been sent in to help. It's tragic, so tragic, and it's only going to get worse, you can count on that. That from the Cassandra on her knees in front of the kitchen stove, trying to scrub away a brown spot that refused to disappear. Once again, somebody had let a hot coal fall out of the stove onto the floor.

Whenever she heard the word "somebody," Christina felt it was intended for her and so immediately tried to change the subject. She asked for particulars about the situation in the city. People returning from their night shifts had offered up additional details. These were embellished as hearsay was passed along from person to person, but the essence of these unconfirmed rumors, stated with complete conviction, was that the city had been reduced to nothing.

Christina hoped that everyone had been inside the bunkers.

Her daughter was acting so responsibly lately, her mother thought, as she watched Christina stand up and put her cup in the sink. Her face with its high cheek bones was pale as always. Christina stroked her left nostril with her index finger, a gesture typical for her when she felt forced to hide her fear. She should dress warmly, as it was drizzling outside.

It was really cold, and Christina was freezing in her windbreaker. She had only herself to blame that she didn't have a proper winter coat. Despite her mother's advice—and ultimately, her warnings—

Christina had sacrificed her last ration coupon for this ridiculous rag. To practical-minded German mothers, "rags" were clothes that served no useful purpose, like, for example, this windbreaker. Christina knew that it was a relic from an earlier time as soon as she spied it in the window of the Huss sporting goods store. Such leftovers used to be considered white elephants, but now they were remnants from another world that the children of the war had only heard about.

"Back then, in those days . . ." was one of the grown-ups' favorite phrases. Their faces lit up, while the children could only listen in disbelief as they described stores filled with all kinds of goods and Sunday dinner tables laden with all kinds of delicacies, like veal kidneys with homemade noodles, and, for dessert, coffee and Frankfurter kringel with real butter crème. They swallowed as their mouths watered.

Back then, for example, there were outfits made entirely out of one kind of cloth, not like nowadays, when they're cobbled together from bits of material left over from someone else's old clothing. Like Christina's Sunday dress: the top part was made out of Oma Stina's old winter dirndl and the skirt from her father's pants, the material turned inside out and pieced together, with a gray border at the hem because she had had another growth spurt.

Her windbreaker was made of beige twill and had a hood with a blue lining. With only that to wear, Christina would freeze to death during the winter, or even worse, she'd probably develop a chronic bladder infection. Although her mother's predictions most often proved correct, it would have seemed to Christina a character defect to admit that her mother was right. So, she suffered in silence. She wrapped her head in her wool scarf and walked along the highway between the fields, the same route she had to take at least twice every day, since she lived on the outskirts of the village.

There was hardly any traffic, just now and then a farmer's tractor and a couple of bicyclists who pedaled wearily and stared straight ahead. Some of their carbide lights were still on and looked like eerie eyes approaching in the rain.

At the cemetery, where Pumpwerkstrasse curved into the main street, she met Ilse Bühler, a classmate from grade school. Ilse launched right in with the latest news. Have you heard? The train station is gone, the asphalt is in flames, and that's where they're going to send us to work. Ilse had plaited her long black hair into a single braid, bound with a brown ribbon that matched her coat. She was not wearing the short, pleated skirt that was the envy of all the village girls. She had on a track suit, since you need to be able to move freely when you're in a work detail.

Ilse was in a hurry. She was always afraid she would miss something. In particular, Walter Zehler, with whom she was madly in love. Like everyone who's in love, she desperately wanted irrefutable evidence that her feelings were reciprocated—something she could find only when she was in his immediate presence. She was already a flirt, something the village mothers took note of. She'll end up just like her mother, who had also started early.

Ilse didn't have a father, at least not one that anyone knew of. Her mother worked as a master seamstress in a corset factory and, by virtue of this position, was among the fortunate who had "connections." Items from the fashionable Felina line of undergarments were often handed over the counter to female shopkeepers in exchange for groceries or whatever else was needed. It was rumored in the village that Ilse's mother also had other "connections," but that was not discussed in Christina's house. Around here we don't gossip about other people.

Everybody's got some dirty linen. That was Elise's motto.

Ilse's mother, Marie, is and always has been a good soul. It was not her fault that she had gotten pregnant by someone who left her in the lurch. In return for her non-judgmental attitude towards the village sinner, Elise also occasionally received a brassiere that had washable stays (patented!), complete with bodice.

Ilse was already wearing a bra, although she had less need for support than Christina. They had compared chests once, and ever since, Christina had tried to more or less flatten out the small swellings by pulling her undershirt tight toward the back and pinning it together with safety pins. She felt absolutely no need to "ripen," as they called this process of maturing, and thereby have to give up all her usual habits. You were also supposed to keep yourself clean, and that was easier said than done when there was no longer any soap to be had. Ilse always had it easier. She somehow managed to get what others could only wish for in vain. For example, the night before, Ilse had gone to see *The Golden City*, a film you had to be eighteen years old to get into. She had cried so hard when, at the end, Kristina Söderbaum had walked off into the moor.

Christina felt a twinge of envy, but immediately forgot it, as Ilse went on to assure Christina that she looked exactly like the movie star. Even though Christina had recently been pinning her hair—à la Söderbaum—up on the top of her head, she blushed and told Ilse that she was imagining things.

The two of them linked arms and walked along the embankment, where the river began to curve and broaden as it flowed toward the village. Across the river, you could see the skyline of the city, with red billowing clouds that thickened into black smoke before disappearing into the rain clouds.

The rain will help put out the fires, Ilse said.

Not the phosphorus fires—they have to be put out with sand.

Now Ilse wanted to know what phosphorus was, and Christina, one of the few village children who had been allowed to go on to Gymnasium, was only too happy to show off her superior knowledge. It's a chemical element, number fifteen on the Periodic Table, and means "light bringing."

Ilse was impressed and passed this information on to those who were already sitting in the trucks in front of City Hall and who, to her dismay, had already claimed the best seats. Do you want to know what phosphorus is?

Christina was not pleased with Ilse's readiness to trade on some- one else's knowledge and pass it off as if it were her own. But she let it go, since just then Walter, dressed in his uniform with shoulder cords indicating his leadership role, directed the latecomers to the last truck and climbed in himself. He handed out the shovels and gave instructions as to what was to happen next.

According to our orders, we're to assemble at the meeting point near the water tower and await further instructions there. Food will be provided. This last bit of information meant that you could now go ahead and eat the jam sandwich you had brought—assuming you had been given one to bring along.

Christina sat in the back of the truck on a sack next to Kurt Keil; the others perched on benches that had been temporarily fastened to the side panels of the truck. Mothers stood in front of the entrance to City Hall, among them Kurt's, who waved to him with her milk can- nister on her arm while he made faces back at her.

The truck's engine, powered by charcoal, belched puffs of smoke into the office of Herr Feuerstein, the town clerk, where today, like every other morning, people were standing in line for ration cards. The boys and girls waved. The mothers in front of City Hall waved back. None of them, not a single one, would have thought to raise any protest against having their children carried off this way into the burning city.

They were off, up the ramp to the bridge, then across the river. On the highway, the truck had to suddenly swerve around a bomb crater. Wow! That must have been a British thousand-pounder—you can even see the groundwater. Necks craned to the left. Those in the know took the opportunity to speculate further. No, you're wrong. That was the Americans with their Flying Fortresses—you could hear them coming. Kurt tried to imitate the droning sound of the plane engines. Gerda made sounds like the fighter planes escorting them. Walter said he thought she sounded more like a cow having a calf. Everybody laughed.

On the highway, those who had been bombed out had loaded their few rescued belongings on small carts and were dragging them to the homeless shelters outside the city. At the edge of the city you could see the first-responding fire department trucks with men in helmets setting up the hoses. Farther in, the burning streets, the sounds of falling beams and crumbling brick walls. When they arrived at the assembly site, brigades were organized. Christina went with her group to the bunker near the municipal tennis courts, whose entrance was blocked with rubble. She shoveled next to a boy from the eastern part of the city. His house had burned down and his sister, who had been slightly injured, was in a Red Cross tent near the water tower. He himself had dragged her out of a hole in the cellar shortly after the phosphorus cannister had hit. The boy, who was thin as a rail, shoveled like a mad man and talked to Christina in the same tempo as he shoveled. His parents had not yet been found, but work to clear the rubble was still underway. The rescue crews had already managed to clear a couple of entrances, but so far had found only shriveled, incinerated corpses.

If Christina had ever been in danger of passing out, it was at the moment when the boy started to classify dead bodies. In a state of complete panic, she dropped her shovel. Then it happened: a rush of air, a feeling of weightlessness, and then a field kitchen flew past her and it started raining lentil soup.

A delayed-action bomb had exploded. Such bombs lie quietly in the dirt and keep ticking in order to kill the survivors who approach with their shovels and then try to run away from the ruins as quickly as possible. Whoever designed this kind of time bomb must have been interested in balancing out the number of casualties. The villagers had to sacrifice some of their own. Ilse was not the first nor would she be the last.

At her burial—there had to be funerals even if the casket was empty—Christina offered up a poem. Casting her eyes toward heaven, she sent Ilse up to wander in the clouds alongside Goethe. *Was ihr fürchtet und auch wohl erlebt, wie's oben drohet, so es unten bebt.*[13]

The mourners gathered around the grave, bowed their heads, and let the words wash over them. In his closing prayer, the pastor entrusted the soul of the departed to God above. Performing his duty, the cemetery keeper gestured to the family members with a small shovel, an opportunity to cast a bit of earth into the grave to officially end the ceremony. But Ilse's mother didn't choose to take part in this ritual. From her sobs there suddenly arose accusations. This damned war! That damned Hitler! Those scoundrels!

The pastor tried to calm Frau Bühler but, unable to do so, handed her over to Christina's mother. Frau Bühler's gaze shot past Elise and along the bowed heads until it came to rest on Christina's face.

Easy for you to talk, Elise, your child is still alive.

It was the word "still" that Christina couldn't forget, all the way to the mortuary where the attendant was laying out the wreaths. Wreaths of fall foliage and evergreen boughs adorned with asters that would cover the mounded earth until it settled. Later, at the wake, they told Christina that Frau Bühler hadn't really meant what she'd

---

[13] In English: *What you fear and also experience, just as it threatens above, it quakes below.* These are the last two lines of the stanza about cumulus clouds in Goethe's poem dedicated to Luke Howard, the English "Classifier of Clouds" (1772-1864), entitled *Howards Ehrengedächtnis (1821).*

said. To make her feel better, they gave Christina an extra piece of cake, which she accepted with some hesitation. An extra piece of cake didn't unsay what had been said. Neither did the plaid pleated skirt that Ilse's mother later gave to Christina, but which she never wore.

Christina had made up her mind to survive, no matter what it took.

Old people—and in those days that included people in their late fifties—seemed to find dying easier than struggling daily for survival. They passed away, one after the other, like Tante Eva, who was found sitting on her garden bench with her hands folded in her lap. Shortly after that, Onkel Karl died too, after falling off his bike on his way home from work and cutting his head open. His condition hadn't seemed too serious at first, but as Onkel Thomas said, he had simply thrown in the towel. Onkel Thomas was the one who had taken over the remainder of Tante Eva's wine business, hoping to get over her death that way. Those two had suffered enough, is what everybody said; they could now rest in peace. The people who were somewhat younger, who would have been in the prime of their lives were it not for the goddamned war, felt that they were the real losers, since the daily tally of all that they had lost now began to include the names of their children.

The trains rolled out of the stations on their way to victory, and mothers waved, and young girls blew kisses, kisses that had been exchanged the night before for hollow promises. You must write, you must come back, promise you'll always love me.

During a game of spin the bottle, Waldemar had given Christina her first kiss, tenderly, carefully, a kiss that tasted of cigarettes. Waldemar, an officer candidate in the Greater Germany Regiment, whose parents had personally dedicated him to the Führer, leaned out the train window and, along with all the others going off to war, reached out his arms as if to embrace those staying behind. The latter ran a few steps alongside the train, as if they wanted to follow, but then stopped and stood still, furtively wiping away their tears.

He kept his promise. He wrote long letters in his almost childish handwriting, first from the training camp in Cottbus and then, after a brief leave before being deployed, from a trench in the vicinity of Schitomir—a city Christina reckoned lay halfway between Stalingrad and Berlin—where three weeks later he died fighting for the Führer, the People, and the Fatherland.

The details of his death were reported to Christina by a fellow soldier who visited when he was home on sick leave. Shot in the neck, Waldemar had not suffered—for which they should all be grateful. Christina hoped it had been a small hole—without any blood if that were possible— and, of course, that he lay in a hero's grave that Russian tanks had not yet rolled over. The soldier, whose words Christina had trouble understanding as they emerged haltingly through the wire contraption holding his lower jaw together, looked on mutely, apparently incapable of sympathy, as Christina broke down in uncontrollable sobs. There hadn't been enough time to actually experience real love; thus, she felt her loss even more deeply. Waldemar remained the ideal, the one everyone else failed to measure up to—those pale young men she didn't want to make love with, partly out of fear, partly as a sign of devotion to her fallen hero.

In Christina's bedroom, her mother wipes away the grit that constantly rains down from the bomb-damaged ceiling onto the hero's shrine—his picture, enlarged and in color so that his deep blue eyes showed, the letters he had written from the field sorted by date, the book he had given her, *The Street Along the River*.[14]

---

[14] *Die Strasse neben dem Strom*, a novella by Andreas Birkner, published 1941.

A major cleaning is also needed at Onkel Werner's, who has been living by himself ever since Tante Lisa fled to the Odenwald, and who will soon be up to his neck in filth. No wonder he has pneumonia and is lying on the chaise lounge in the kitchen, drenched in sweat and gasping for air. The cold compresses don't seem to be doing any good, and they're worried that he's been in this condition going on nine days—usually that's when the crisis comes. He keeps insisting that he doesn't want to be a burden to Elise, while she rubs his pale, hairy legs with alcohol, moving upward from his ankles toward his heart, bypassing his privates, which she has tried to cover with a washcloth. Nobody is going to die here, not as long as she's in charge!

But his fever rises, and Onkel Werner tries to get up. It's all Christina's mother can do to hold down the patient who is desperate for air and wants to go outside, where he certainly would catch his death. They can't get him into the air-raid shelter anymore when the sirens go off, so they have to stay up top with him, cowering and hoping that, if there is any justice in the world, today the planes will unload their bombs somewhere else.

But there is no justice. With every bomb explosion Onkel Werner rises up like Lazarus from his pillow, only to be pushed back down by four arms. Through the half-open sliding door, you can see lightning-like flashes in the living room, and broken glass from the windows shatters noisily onto the floor. A crack the width of a finger slowly creeps up the wall next to the kitchen cupboard, and a gust of wind makes the kitchen light sway. Christina's mother invokes God's name in a tone bordering on blasphemy, wondering how in the world He could be letting this happen. Here lies a critically ill man who has never hurt a fly. She really lets Him have it, while again placing a compress on Onkel Werner's chest. For a moment, Christina thinks her mother has snapped—until she sees her run into Tante Lisa's living room, armed with a dustpan and whisk broom, and start to sweep up the broken glass. She's back to normal!

You'd have died laughing, Christina would say afterwards, describing the scene in her usual ebullient style. Mother is sweeping up just as the second wave of bombers is about to attack.

But it won't be a laughing matter to Tante Lisa, who's got a guilty conscience for having left Onkel Werner to fend for himself at such a difficult time. After all, it was her husband, teetering on the brink of death, who has played the starring role in this mini-drama.

Onkel Werner's breathing sounds like a steam engine. Completely exhausted, he can only wave his arms about and mutter random words that never make any sense. In contrast, there is the constant drone of engines whose sounds make perfectly clear what's about to happen. Christina sits under the kitchen table and picks at a worn spot in the linoleum floor.

She will later accept responsibility for the hole in the linoleum, but no one will take responsibility for the hole in the attic. A phosphorus bomb has hit the house and the rescue squad, alerted by the neighbors, bangs on the front door. OPEN UP! FIRE!

Luckily, there's a bucket of water and several pails of sand in the stairwell. At the end of the bucket brigade stands Christina's mother, who keeps the supply coming thanks to a pile of sand near the entrance.

Christina's solution? Take cover! But where? And preferably not alone.

Under the cellar steps along with Greif, the building watchdog, who bites? Not there, for sure.

Next door at the Heierlings! But unfortunately, their attic is already in flames and they are trying to rescue anything that can still be saved. Christina rescues all twelve volumes of Becker's *World History* as well as a Wilhelm Busch album. The firemen, unable to keep up with the consequences of the daily incineration, don't arrive until the Heierling's house has already burned down to the ground floor.

Is everybody safe? Thanks for asking, replies Frau Heierling, sitting on a Persian carpet under her sourcherry tree, surrounded by what's left of her belongings. She will give Becker's *World History* to Christina, who, the next day, places the volumes—many of them soaked during the attempt to douse the fire—in the sunshine, turning and reading each page, one after the other, as they dry. Her avid interest in history, particularly the history of the Romans, must have been sparked at that time, since it was precisely the third volume—Roman history up to the time of Constantine—that had suffered the most water damage.

From then on, she would talk shop with Onkel Werner, who had been schooled in the classics and was now well on his way to recovery. And before long, Professor Hawner began to call upon Fräulein Steiger whenever questions arose regarding specific dates in ancient history.

It apparently never occurred to her at the time that everything happening right then was also part of history. Later on, she'd be able to read about it in history books, and she could even take issue with what she read: No, it didn't happen like that!

The battle of Stalingrad, for example, later always considered by historians to have been the turning point in the war, only took on special meaning for Christina because Frau Pfeifer, who had been bombed out and had taken refuge in the Späther's washhouse, had both a son and a husband in this battle. Since it was always bitter cold in the washhouse, she often came to the Steigers to warm up and at the same time get things off her chest. Even when it was announced that a new machine gun was being deployed that could fire three thousand rounds per minute, her fears about the situation around Stalingrad were not allayed. She closely followed the army reports and fretted about her two men, who purportedly had to endure awful conditions because they were encircled and could no longer be adequately supplied by air. Christina's mother suggested that maybe things weren't quite that bad. Oh, Frau Steiger, they're freezing, and they're starving. The Späthers, whose only concern at the moment was the impending reduction in meat rations for those who kept rabbits, were less than sympathetic, lamented Frau Pfeifer. While the defenders of Stalingrad were confined in close quarters in the southern and middle parts of the city and engaged in heroic resistance—as announced by the Office of the Supreme Army Command, according to Frau Pfeifer—the Späthers were slaughtering their rabbits in order to avoid having to pay the recently announced general tax on livestock. In the spring, Frau Späther discovered that someone had stolen her rabbit pelts. Frau Pfeifer's loss was greater. Her son had been killed and her husband taken prisoner. The battle of Stalingrad thus remained, in Christina's mind, Frau Pfeifer's slaughter.

The slaughter at El Alamein, on the other hand, belonged to Heinz, Tante Eva's second foster son, a career soldier who had left home a long time ago. Christina knew him only in uniform, smartly turned out, always with a girl on his arm. He was in the Africa Corps and was in fact a messenger for a general. As Tante Eva knew from his letters, he drove a BMW motorcycle across the desert. On one such mission, he drove by mistake into a British outpost, which brought an abrupt end to his military career. Tante Eva defended him by claiming that something like that could easily happen since there were no signposts in the desert. But he was treated well and humanely in the British prisoner-of-war camp.

The battle of Charkov—that is, the brief recapture of this city in the spring of '43—was credited to her father, although he definitely would have been loath to accept such an honor. In any case, his entire unit except for him and one other man was lost in the vicinity of this city. For days, the two survivors wandered around the region until a mopping-up squad rescued the half-starved comrades and delivered them to a supply depot. It was only later, after the war, that Christina learned from the other surviving soldier that he and her father had been part of a "suicide squad"—namely a unit composed of purported enemies of the state who were considered no more than cannon fodder. In any event, the two men ended up in the supply depot, where they were given clerical jobs and fattened up. Christina's father came home on his first leave from the front well nourished. He even brought along a large packet of food that he had been given when he crossed the border. He brought a balalaika for Christina that he had bought from a Russian. Bought, he repeated, for emphasis.

There were lots of visitors when he was home on leave. All the relatives seemed to want to hear from Philipp how he thought things would end. Survive, he said, just survive, and only then will we be able to tell how things will go.

This was easier said than done.

People who equated defeat in the war with annihilation vowed to carry on until the bitter end. If worse came to worst, the way out was the last bullet, the one you had left when all else had failed. Walter Zehler, who—as he let Christina know—had distinguished himself at the battle of Tarnopol, belonged to this faithful-until-death group. The two of them were sitting in the Café Schneider drinking ersatz coffee and trying to pierce an unyielding crust of frosted dough with a pastry fork. Walter in his Waffen-SS[15] uniform, she in the uniform of a streetcar conductor, that is, a Gymnasium student assigned to duty on the homefront.

---

[15] The military division of the Nazi Party's SS (Schutzstaffel=Protection Forces) organization. (simple.wikipedia/org/wiki/Waffen-SS)

Dear Miss Conductor, ding, ding, ding! Tell us where the tram is going, ding, ding, ding!

From the radio on the counter came the first report from the field about the invasion on the western front. Walter asked the waiter to turn up the volume. The report was devoured by all the café patrons, while their so-called "pastry slices" remained untouched on their plates. Walter did not know much about the situation in the West; he was not allowed to talk about the situation in the East. He was shipping out the next day. Take care of yourself, okay? Of course.

So it was, so it is, so it shall be. Always the same route, past City Hall, down Schlossstrasse, at the same hour, at the same pace, looking down at the ground. Now occasionally glancing to the right over to the fence surrounding a prison camp that had recently been built to house the forced laborers who worked in a factory that had been relocated here from somewhere in the city. Sometimes she saw a man's face, sometimes a hand on the fence that might later squeeze through the bars to hang there, open. One morning she happened to walk on the other side of the street. As she came closer to the open hand, she took her lunch sandwich out of her pocket and put it in the hand.

She hadn't thought anything of it, she would later say, when, at City Hall, she had to justify her behavior. As she well knew, there was a law against fraternization. The scholar in her told the official that a piece of dry bread simply given away like that could hardly be considered an attempt at fraternization. Oh, so you're a smart mouth as well, retorted the functionary.

At the next troop meeting, Group Leader Titti asks Christina to step to the door, pulls off her neckerchief with its woven leather knot and her red and white ribbon, and dismisses her from the group. The rumor that she had had dealings with one of the prisoners, in broad daylight no less, was the talk of the village for weeks.

Christina had always admired people who were capable of disregarding the rules without losing more than they gained. This was a trait she had never been able to acquire because of all the years she had spent being trained to be obedient. Only now did she realize how much she depended on the approval of others. To be sure, she could just shrug her shoulders and turn to those who would forgive what she had done. But that wouldn't put the matter to rest. The burning issue remained: how could she, how could I? It was not just a question; she was questioning her very being.

Recompense: revenge for some affront suffered or the repayment of a favor?

"God will repay you," Sister Fakunda said as she took a couple of roofing tiles from the Steiger storehouse to repair the roof of her Catholic convent. God would have to provide recompense to Christina, since Sister Fakunda didn't have any money.

There was another kind of recompense that people were supposed to believe in these days—namely, payback defined in simple, numerical terms. This kind of retribution had been enthusiastically embraced after the major air attacks during the summer of '43. What other options were there when anti-aircraft fire and nightly sorties of fighter planes had no effect? Out of Christian charity, Sister Fakunda would have had to foreswear thoughts of this sort of recompense, but the general population wanted nothing more than for the Tommies to get a taste of their own medicine. Misery loves company.

After the Allied invasion, it was rumored that the enemies on the western front had intentionally been allowed to gain a foothold so that they could be definitively wiped out by means of a new weapon, the V1. Herr Doktor Bender, the rather sclerotic physics professor called back out of retirement, talked a lot of nonsense about guided missiles loaded with at least five thousand kilograms of explosive, that is, a weapon of retribution of the most lethal caliber. There were other claims about a winged, bomb-carrying rocket loaded with liquid oxygen that could be programmed to fly a specific distance. People were also wracking their brains speculating about the V2. Peter Schmidt, a classmate whose father was a naval officer, claimed to have overheard that there were miniature submarines that were impossible for enemy sonar to detect. Christina pinned her hopes on an anti-aircraft gun with a directional antenna that could find its target with deadly accuracy. Once, she thought that such a device must already exist—namely, when she was able to witness the first daylight bombing raid on the city from a hilltop twenty kilometers away. One plume of smoke after another descended out of the clouds, and her heart beat faster and faster as she began to count them. It turned out later that they had only been target-marking bombs.

If you really want to know what the future holds, you can go see the fortune-teller, who has set herself up in a little garden house down at the end of Wasserstrasse. In exchange for a little bit of food, Gerda has already been told that her father would come back home.

And? What else? Gerda was beaming. She'd been told that she, too, would survive the war. Gerda had earned it—this momentary glimpse into the future—and you couldn't help but be a little envious of her for that. From now on, it would be smart to stick close to her in the bunker since the immediate vicinity around her would probably offer some protection. But going to visit the fortune-teller on her own was something Christina never got up the nerve to do.

It's probably just nonsense, Frau Bühler confided to Elise, who told Frau Späther, who would then pass it on to Gerda's mother. But maybe there is something to it, since the fortune-teller's prediction that Lenni Hartmann would get into trouble by constantly being around men had come true. Lenni was going to have a baby. Did anybody know which of the anti-aircraft gunners was the father? None of them. She had gotten pregnant by a laborer from the East and therefore had had all of her hair cut off. Christina unconsciously neatened her braids that had been smoothed with sugar water and pinned up with hairpins in the latest war-time fashion.

Christina is drawn to Lenni as a kindred spirit. She had never been up to Lenni's attic room over the store. In the stairwell it smells like a warehouse, although the cartons and boxes that are stacked up in the storage rooms on the first floor all seem to be empty. No, Christina notices that there is a crate of Persil laundry soap that is still half full, but she doesn't give in to the temptation to steal a box of it. They might accuse Lenni of that. At the top landing there is a door with a nameplate on it: Marlene Hartmann, in Gothic script no less.

After several knocks, the door opens. There's Lenni in her house-coat and kerchief, boiling her laundry on the stove and stirring the wash kettle with a large wooden paddle so that it doesn't boil over. A damp, unpleasant odor of drying laundry and un-aired bed linens hits Christina in the face. Lenni, apparently glad to see her, offers her unexpected guest a seat. Christina doesn't want Lenni to go to any trouble. What she wants, but can't admit, is for Lenni to take off her kerchief. Lenni will not do her this favor. Instead, she takes out of her pillowcase a photo that shows her and a hollow-cheeked man holding each other close, standing in front of a brick wall with a "No Parking" sign on it.

She would marry him as soon as this whole mess is over with. And it won't take all that much longer. She figures three months, so by spring the war will be over.

In January, on the way home from her night shift, Lenni went into labor. They found her doubled up in pain in the plum orchard where the embankment slopes rather steeply down to the river. The child lived for a week, Lenni three weeks longer. Her red hair shone brightly through the white chrysanthemums that encircled her head. At the mortuary, Christina was on the lookout for the prospective bridegroom, but he was nowhere to be seen. Lots and lots of villagers, on the other hand, thronged around Lenni's coffin, paying her their last respects. The departed was immediately forgiven all her sins.

Which is worse, being cold or being hungry?

Being hungry, for sure.

Being hungry meant that Christina had to agree to go with her friend Maria Seitz on a scavenging trip to the Odenwald. Maria had an uncle there who owned a farm, and who was thus in a position to barter for all kinds of things on the black market. Elise reluctantly parted with her set of Rosenthal china that could be exchanged for a packet of pipe tobacco and fifty cigarettes, which could in turn be traded for something else. Gerda took the last two bottles of cognac from her father's liquor cabinet, and Maria hoped her uncle would just give her a little something without expecting anything in return.

They had a headwind against them, so it was very slow going. Maria, who was riding her father's bicycle and could barely reach the pedals, rubbed her rear end raw on the saddle. Gerda got side stitches and had to rest for a while on top of one of the stone kilometer markers. Christina kept urging them on; she really wanted to get the last stretch of the trip on the open highway over with as quickly as possible, since once they reached the forest they'd be safer from the low-flying fighter planes, which lately had begun strafing individuals spotted on the road.

Things were peaceful in Waldbrunn, their destination for the day-long journey. At least there was the sense here that things were still as they used to be. Next to Onkel Karle's house there was a steaming manure pile with clucking chickens scratching around. There was an aroma of . . . onion tart, announced Maria, ditching her bike next to the front steps and running into the house, following the aroma. Gerda and Christina stood uneasily with their bicycles in the courtyard until young Karle came out, looked them over from head to foot, then asked them to come in. Christina didn't care for onion tart, but she gladly accepted a liverwurst sandwich. In fact, two, then a third. She would prefer to get the negotiations underway quickly, since young Karle's suggestive comments gave her the distinct impression that he had his mind set on an exchange of favors that she was not prepared to engage in.

He'd like a hug and a squeeze, this farmer's boy, in exchange for a ham. Maria asked why not? Not for everything hanging in the smokehouse! What's worse—going hungry or getting squeezed? If that's as far as it goes, commented Gerda, who for safety's sake had already bolted the door shut and climbed into bed with all her clothes on. I'd rather go hungry, Christina said, just before dropping off to sleep. But that was easy to say on a full stomach.

On the way home the next day, Maria's sister met them at the canal bridge bearing the bad news that Gerda's mother had fallen down the bunker steps and injured her back. And in addition, Christina's father had come home yesterday on leave! Christina made it from the bridge to her house in record time. When she got there, she unpacked ham and sausage and bread from her rucksack and laid everything out on the table in front of her father as if it were a sacrificial offering.

Does he want something to eat? No, he wants to take her in his arms; he wants to give her a big hug. So he had not really forgotten her, even though he had mentioned her only briefly in his letters: she should be a good girl, support her mother, not cause him any worries.

Nobody ever asked them—the ones on leave—how long they could stay. You would just find yourself unpleasantly surprised when they appeared in the morning, back in their grey uniforms with their bags packed. But only three days? That was too short. And did troop transport trains really leave in the middle of the night? Was there something strange going on here? No, he just had to leave. It was urgent. I'll be back again once it's all over, he promises Christina, cross my heart! And when will that be? Soon. A few weeks at most. And like a visitor shaking hands goodbye, he takes her hand, clasps it tightly, and only when he lets it go does she discover the slip of paper. With a quick motion she reaches under her left arm and hides it in her armpit. Holding her left arm close as if it were in a sling, she uses her right arm to take the packet of food from the table and hands it to her father without looking at him. She has the feeling that she should say something, such as "Take care!" or "See you soon," but she can't find any words appropriate to this nighttime scene.

She watches her father walk through the garden gate, his gait unmistakable, not long strides, more like quick, light steps, conspicuously swinging his arms, his upper body bent slightly forward as if he were bracing against the wind.

Falling asleep was out of the question after this, even though there was not yet any sign of night turning into day. Her mother was poking the fire in the stove, laying some kindling on the embers and putting on water for tea.

Just sitting around and waiting. Asking her mother for some kind of explanation is out of the question. Christina becomes aware of her hand holding the slip of paper. She gets the idea of going into the WC only after drinking two cups of linden blossom tea.

"Sandhausen, Uferweg 3." She memorizes the address and flushes the piece of paper down the toilet.

When they came the next morning to take her father away, they ended up leaving empty-handed. But no one slips through their net, you could be sure of that. Hatred, pure hatred, that was what Christina felt for the first time in her life. She knew exactly what these scoundrels were up to. They wanted to kill her father, the father who overnight had become perfect—her mother could only remember his good qualities. He always took care of us, right? He was a good man, he had his heart in the right place. He would never hurt a fly. It bothered Christina that they were talking about him in the past tense. He's going to come back. Soon. Let's hope so!

Sandhausen, Uferweg 3. There lay hope, hope she could reach in an hour on her bike. Even quicker on Gerda's bike instead of her old clunker. But Gerda needed her bike. Her mother was doing very poorly. Her pain was so unbearable that a doctor had to come see her. She was going to die slowly, from the bottom up. Christina thought of the yellow plum tree in the garden, whose dead branches had only managed to sprout a few green leaves last spring. It won't bear again, declared her mother, it's dying.

Although Christina resisted, Gerda insisted on showing her what she meant when she talked about her mother's dying. She pulled the reluctant Christina into the bedroom where her mother, Emma, lay, tickled the soles of her feet and pinched her calves, but the patient reacted only with a dismissive hand motion, as if she wanted to be done with life, the life that Gerda so forcefully clung to. Which is worse, to lose a father or a mother? The worst thing is that children should even have to ask such questions. Still pondering this, Gerda nonetheless falls asleep—Gerda, the half-orphan with whom Christina will share her bed from now on. Her bed, yes, but not the dream that awakens Christina in the middle of the night. She was walking down a country road. In front of her were figures with their backs turned toward her, although they were recognizable from their posture and the way they walked. Whenever Christina tried to catch up with them, they would walk faster. She called them by name, but they didn't stop. She ran faster and faster, gasping desperately for air, grabbed hold of one by the belt, and suddenly they were face to face. Then she realized with indescribable horror that where there was supposed to be a face, there was only a blank surface, and when she cried out "It's me, it's me!" the entire figure dissolved into itself until it completely disappeared.

There was no house at No. 3 Uferweg. There was a filling station that was no longer in business, but in the service bay an older man in a blue coverall was tinkering with the engine housing of a Zündapp motorcycle. In response to Christina's inquiring look, he explained that there were no replacement parts anymore. Yes, she knew that, her father had an old Opel standing in his workshop, and it wouldn't run properly either. What's your father's name? Philipp Steiger. Christina held her breath, thinking that now what would happen would be what she had so often imagined. Someone would take her by the hand and lead her into a back room, where her father, smoking a cigarette, would be resting on a cot waiting for the war to be over.

But no such thing. The man was not the owner of the service station; he was just allowed to work on his motorcycle there. The owner is not here. He works during the day at the armament works, in the cable factory in Waldorf. His name is Bertold, Jakob Bertold. He lives around back where they've added on. His wife is dead, his son in the Panzer Corps, missing for a year. Too bad about the son; he was supposed to take over the business. Jakob is a good man, has his heart in the right place. Another good man. Christina was glad to hear that. Did that mean that the "right" place was a little more toward the left?

Sandhausen was a row village. The houses were all built along the main street and the street that ran parallel to it along the river-bank. Christina wandered back and forth between the two streets until it was dark. Then she sat on an oil drum behind the service station waiting for the light to come on in the addition. In February it got dark early. The church bell struck half-past, then quarter-to. That was the trouble with church bells: you never knew exactly what time it was until it tolled the full hour. And if you didn't begin counting right when it started, you had to wait another whole hour to find out what time it was. That's why we have pocket watches, kitchen clocks, grandfather clocks. But here, under the corrugated metal overhang that offered precious little protection from the cold rain, the church bell was all there was.

It was six o'clock. From an open window of the neighboring house, she could hear music on the radio. A request-program medley of tunes from Lehar's *Der Zarewitsch*. Christina slowly began to cry. The main reason for this emotional outburst was not her sympathy for the poor soldier on the Volga who was hoping for an angel, but more likely because her legs and feet had become numb from the cold and dangled from the oil drums as if they no longer belonged to her.

She had to go home, having accomplished nothing. Once she got home, she'd have to tell lies again, lies that—contrary to folk wisdom—would serve her well and get her out of any predicament: I was over at my classmate Erich's house cramming, and we completely lost track of the time. Why was she always hanging out with the boys? Because there are only three girls in the whole school, and I can't study with any of them, except maybe Gudrun, but she lives with her grandmother in the turret of an old mansion, and the old lady doesn't like having visitors. Erich's parents, on the other hand, are very nice, really nice. Christina chattered on like that until she and her mother were both awash in a sea of everyday trivialities. You don't say! How could her mother know that the daughter who stood there leaning against the wall next to the warm stove had feet that were almost frostbitten and hurt so much that she was about to faint?

Oatmeal cooked with sugar, cinnamon, and milk, what kind of supper is that? Gerda, always the accepting sort, thought they ought to be thankful that there was still something to eat. If Christina wants something better, then she ought to go to the railroad yard in Blumenau where, since yesterday, army supply trains have been sitting, loaded with provisions for the troops. And since the bombed-out section of track has not yet been repaired, there's looting going on. What kind of stuff is there? Everything you can think of! This is an opportunity worth playing hooky for. A sideways glance over the pile of clothes needing mending, where her mother is using tiny cross stitches to sew a new seam into a pair of underpants. Torn between her role as guardian of an orderly household and that of a sole provider whose sources were slowly drying up, Elise suggests that perhaps they can discuss this in the morning. But this doesn't dampen Christina's excited anticipation. Anticipation, the unleashing of endless possibilities! Gerda should make a list. Bread, of course. Artificial honey and canned meat. French cognac by the case! Good for exchanging on the black market, not for them to drink. Agreed!

It was pitch black when they started out. Trudging across the fields, they clambered over the frozen clumps of earth. They had to stop often so that Christina could fix the boot that she had wrapped in rags. The boot had a large hole in the sole where slush would seep in if you weren't careful to keep the spot tightly covered. The main tracks leading to the south switching yard ran alongside the Blumenau woods, which used to be a destination for nature lovers but was now closed off to the public with barbed wire and "No

Trespassing" signs. Through the pine trees you could make out the shape of the Panzer crews' barracks, and Christina reckoned the men were already having breakfast. She sniffed the air until she had the whole menu figured out. Coffee, of course, definitely coffee. And cocoa. And rolls, warm rolls with butter and marmalade. You can't smell marmalade, Gerda teased, as she danced along the rails as if she were a high-wire artiste. She carefully placed one foot in front of the other and balanced herself with outstretched arms, from which fluttered the pillowcases that were meant to be used later as carrying bags. Ladies and Gentlemen, the amazing Gerda Martin! It was Christina who heard the train coming and who shouted "take cover" as loud as she could, since she couldn't think of anything better to say. They tumbled down the embankment and landed in each other's arms in the ditch. And here came the guardian angel, flying by like a sparrow-hawk, pulling the train cars past them, once again giving Christina proof of Gerda's indestructibility.

At the railroad junction they met two women pushing bicycles loaded down with sacks. It wasn't much farther. The best stuff was in the front cars, but some people were already fighting over things up there. Those who were less desperate were busy taking things from the cars at the back. Some of them even gave the girls some things from their sacks as soon as they came across something better. Gerda and Christina did the same. Put it in the sack, take it back out of the sack. That way you had the feeling later on that you hadn't missed anything.

What's more important, toothpaste or bouillon cubes? Bouillon cubes, of course, unless we also find toothbrushes.

A lot of stuff had already been taken, and you had to be satisfied with things that other people had rejected. Half a loaf of bread, for instance, that had a few bites missing, but so what. Two bottles with the labels missing, little bags of dried peas, some cans without labels but with letters and numbers stamped on them. Christina took a chance on something labeled "Ö 35," shook it, weighed it in her hands, decided it must be oil. A heavy-set woman, who kept bumping Christina in the ribs with the large rucksack on her back without ever apologizing, offered Christina a tin of what she claimed to be cooking oil in exchange for the bread. The woman would surely have started bargaining if somebody hadn't yelled "Planes!" Trains were the airplanes' favorite targets; they should have thought of that. Time to drop everything and take cover under the cars. Not on your life! Christina didn't leave anything behind. First she dragged her sack under the train and then Gerda, who had gotten caught on the coupling between the cars.

Ami, Ami, fly away, you don't want us anyway. Better go and bomb Berlin, it's them who made the mess we're in.

The fusillade from the planes kicked up little spurts of sand. Inside the train car, Christina's trading partner was moaning. Hampered by her oversized rucksack, she had not been able to get herself through the door opening and had taken cover inside the car. Christina kept on singing, with Gerda singing along in harmony. *This will all soon pass away, every December is followed by May.*

Another round of bullets. Then nothing. The leaden silence of waiting. Amid the silence inside the car, the groans of those who had been wounded. We've got to get out of here. Across the frozen fields until they heard the thin, metallic whine of a plane, then lying down flat in a furrow, their sacks over their heads, wishing they could stay buried there for the winter until everything was over with.

It was only when they got to the road and had taken refuge in the ditch alongside it that Christina noticed the red stains on Gerda's coat. Terrified by what she saw and pointing repeatedly with her index finger at Gerda's chest, she turned her head to the side and threw up.

But it wasn't blood, it was French Bordeaux trickling out of Gerda's breast pocket. They started to laugh, quietly at first, then louder, until they were dancing around in the roadside ditch, doubled over from laughter.

Later they said they had laughed so hard they cried, but whether what they had wiped from their faces were tears of laughter was a matter of debate. There was no clear-cut difference between joy and sorrow for either of them; the distinction had disappeared long ago. They could still laugh, nevertheless, when it turned out that the cans did not contain cooking oil but rather machine oil, and that Gerda had found toothbrushes after all, but they had not kept the toothpaste. They were now brushing their teeth with the soft soap that Christina had picked up at the last moment, God only knows why! It was only the adults, cocooned in their old habits, who were still able to decide whether something was worth crying over or laughing at.

For example, you didn't cry when your bike had a flat tire. Why did Christina always have to be riding somewhere? Where did she have to go now? To Sandhausen, Christina would have liked to reply. But this she couldn't divulge. In response to her questions about where her father might be, she never got a straight answer, or even an informative one. Her mother tried her best to gently suggest that, until the war was over, there would be little hope of any news.

Before it was all over, the crocuses were blooming in the garden. Grass had even grown over the bunker, and a few daisies from the meadow had transplanted themselves into the yard. The willow catkins that Christina had brought home and stuck in the pots of tulips were from Sandhausen, but you couldn't really tell by looking at them. From the attic, where Christina had set up camp in order to spy on the enemy tanks through the holes in the roof tiles, she could only see the branches and twigs of the small yellow plum tree that once again wanted to bloom but struggled to do so. And just when it had finally managed to bring forth a few buds on its top branches, it was blown to bits. It was not on account of the plum tree—which, in any case, was dying—but because of the damaged windows and roofs, that the commanding officer of the bridge demolition squad and Christina—supported by the neighbors whose houses had been damaged by the explosion—got into an argument. The young lieutenant, who had a hard time keeping a straight face, muttered something to the effect that he had only been following orders. Did he really think that that would stop the Americans? He didn't seem to have an opinion one way or the other. Frau Klein, on the other hand, who always had a sense of foreboding that the worst was about to happen, was of the opinion that this was the beginning of the end.

Days stretched like rubber bands to their full lengths, then snapped back into nights during which those exhausted from waiting could only doze, half awake. Once again Christina rode to Sandhausen, so that she could slip a letter under Herr Bertold's door, asking him to get in touch with her.

Herr Bertold never came. What came was a crumpled-up note thrown through her window bearing the news that Herr B. had been arrested and that nothing was known about the fate of comrade S.

What also came was the sound of approaching artillery fire. Then everything was quiet. In order not to disturb this silence, everybody was whispering. Christina lay on the attic floor and kept watch with binoculars. Gerda reported on the situation to those down below: All quiet on the Western Front.

Later, half asleep, Christina heard someone crying. She felt warm. The air in the cellar had gotten muggy. She could barely breathe. Something was stuck in her throat. She couldn't swallow. Terrified, she screamed. A flashlight came on, and in its beam of light, Elise found her daughter who, with tears streaming down her face, whispered pleadingly, over and over, that it was not her fault. Christina held out her arms as if she were drowning, embraced her mother's emaciated torso, and clung to her as if for dear life, while her mother slowly remembered how to hug a child.

"There they are! Look, here they come," Gerda cried and poked Christina hard in the ribs so that they both almost fell off the overturned sauerkraut crock they were perched on in order to see out of the cellar window. They had first spotted the head of the tank column five days ago on the other side of the river, but since both bridges to the village had been blown up, the tanks had detoured around it. They'll just ignore us and let us starve to death, Elise had said, once again predicting the worst. Better a terrible end than unending terror.

Frau Klein, whose imagination with regard to the impending terror ran to thoughts of murder and mayhem, had slipped through the emergency exit back into her own cellar so that she could, as she put it, prepare herself for the worst.

It won't be all that bad, Fritz Nagel had explained, the Amis would build a pontoon bridge as soon as the front had moved farther to the east. Fritz, who had been a member of the Hitler Pioneers[16] before he lost his left leg at the battle of Kuban-Brückenkopf, was considered to be the village expert in modern warfare. Strategically speaking, our village is unimportant. What one wouldn't have given to be certain of that—just a single verifying fact—during these last few days, when waiting from one hour to the next had become increasingly unbearable.

But now they did come, sauntering along both sides of Hindenburgstrasse, past the empty craters where buildings had once stood.

---

[16] Likely a reference to the older (16-17) Hitler Jugend boys who were conscripted into a special division of the Waffen-SS to fight in a number of battles beginning in 1943.

They kept coming, with rifles slung casually over their shoulders, their steel helmets pushed back onto their necks. Their uniforms were not grey, but dusty brown, and they wore high lace-up boots with rubber soles.

Then finally their faces came into focus. A tall, broad-shouldered giant kept rhythmically moving his lower jaw as if he wanted to stifle his laughter. A freckled soldier with short, thick legs stood in front of the Steiger's gate but didn't seem to notice the sign that had been made just for him.

"This house is inhabitated" was written on it in black Gothic script that had been somewhat washed away by the rain. The author of this sentence—one that was displayed on every door on Hindenburgstrasse—was hanging out of the cellar window with Gerda and trying in her best school English to inform the Amis that "all German soldiers are gone hence."

The heads of the residents slowly began to appear over the gates and hedges and from behind windows. Waving a white sheet on a broom handle, an arm thrust itself between two soldiers who quickly ducked for cover. There were no gunshots. "Anybody here speak English?" one of them asked, and Christina climbed out of the cellar window, once again announcing that she would serve as interpreter.

"I tell you all," she said to the soldier, who had five chevrons on his sleeve and an oval patch that showed an axe on a red background. He looked her over from head to foot while she tried to activate her entire English vocabulary, since she knew all the neighbors would be watching her closely and would report the whole scene to the entire world.

"How old are you, Frollein?"

"Seventeen."

"Tell them it's all over. Fini! Verstehen?"

It was peacetime, and those who were to be thanked for bringing it about had in the meantime put up a huge tent on the subdivision's commons and had taken over all the best houses. Flush toilets must have been the deciding factor for the soldiers in choosing their quarters, because the Steigers, whose little place could hardly compete with the fancier houses located farther down Hindenburgstrasse, but who had undertaken to modernize their WC shortly before the war started, were among the unfortunate. On the other hand, the Späthers were spared since, in their house, the water for flushing was still kept in a pail that stood next to the toilet.

The ones who were evicted found lodging with relatives or with neighbors. Christina stayed with her mother in the Späther's washhouse, Frau Pfeifer having graciously ceded it to them because it was high time she looked up her own relatives. People went back to their home villages so that the returning soldiers—and Frau Pfeifer fully expected her husband to be one of them—would not suffer the shock of finding themselves standing in front of a locked door. That she no longer had a door seemed not to have crossed her mind.

From the roof of the washhouse, Christina and Gerda observed the routines of the occupying troops. GI underwear, billowed by the wind, fluttered from the Steiger's second-story balcony, looking like dusty brown sails in the soft breeze. They do seem to be clean, her mother said, clinging to the unspoken hope that the soldiers would keep her house in some semblance of order. She would only too gladly have gone inside to check on things, but fraternizing was strictly prohibited; any contact between the occupying forces and the German citizenry was considered a violation of military code.

Despite this rule, one of the soldiers tried to demonstrate his German proficiency. "Hey, Frolleins," he called to the two swallows on the roof, "Meine Name ist Raoul Marquis und ich bin von Kalifornia." "*Mein* Name," Christina corrected, and was rewarded with a bar of Sweetheart soap. Later there were chocolates, ground coffee in old envelopes, and when he left, a bag full of rations along with his address. He did not get the goodbye kiss he wanted.

When they were allowed back into their house, Christina noticed that all the doors were standing open. In America they must have drapes hanging in their doorways, ventured Christina's mother, the woman who expected the worst and got it. There were dirty bed linens lying everywhere, and from the looks of the mattresses, the Americans had ended up sleeping on them without any sheets. There was not a lot missing. In fact, they found the remains of bars of soap, toothbrushes that had hardly been used, and K-rations, cans with contents that were sometimes known, sometimes unknown. While Gerda helped Christina's mother drag the mattresses into the yard to scrub them with soapy water, Christina snooped around looking for whatever food the Amis had left behind. The aroma coming from the light brown remains in one can encouraged her to risk tasting it. Christina let the first spoonful of the gooey stuff slowly melt in her mouth, then greedily spooned in the remainder until the can was empty. It didn't take long before she felt nauseous. After she vomited, she lay in misery on the kitchen floor while letting it be known that she was about to die. "*Gift!*"[17] screamed her mother, holding the empty can under the nose of the American medical orderly whom Gerda had fetched from the main tent. "Yes, a gift," he confirmed to Elise as he put his cool hand on Christina's sweaty forehead. "And he's even admitting it! I can't believe it!" cried Elise. "No, not German *Gift*, English 'gift'—a present!" Christina translated, as she tried

---

[17] The German word for "poison."

to swallow the giant tablets the orderly had produced from his medical bag and which were intended to alleviate the effects of an overdose of American peanut butter on her malnourished stomach.

The occupying troops gradually left the village, and even more gradually, the returnees began appearing. Her father was not among them. And without him, it didn't seem possible to start over. He would have been the only one able to tell them how everything was supposed to be different now. Things were already different, according to Tante Lisa. We've got that old Socialist Bühler as our mayor, and the important Nazis are in a camp near Stuttgart being sorted out and interrogated. And when Philipp gets back, he can fix my roof right away because it's leaking, and there's already mold in the attic.

Christina's mother had once again hung her husband's clothes in the garden to air out and be brushed off since they still smelled like the cellar and mothballs. A fortune is hanging out there on the clothesline; you could get through this first year of peace in high style with what those clothes would fetch. But Christina's mother won't hear of letting Christina barter a single piece of clothing. Tante Lisa, on the other hand, carries on an active exchange with the Americans, who have taken over the Vetter's large house next door to her and turned it into their Officers Club. As souvenirs for the Amis, she sews swastika flags out of bed sheets that have been dyed red—for which she gets cigarettes, the new currency with which you can buy almost anything on the black market. She needs food, particularly for her Ernst August, who had been drafted into the army during the last days of the war, then sent back home half starved. She still smokes, but since she is now burning up money, she has limited herself to five Lucky Strikes a day.

Gerda's father, Fritz, has come back, and everybody shares her joy, as well as the food he unpacks from his rucksack. He is most appreciative that Elise has taken care of Gerda, and he promises to make it up to her. The former businessman becomes expert at dealing on the black market. Late at night he goes into the city to the train station, where he makes his deals, in particular with the foreigners who work for the Americans in supervised work-crews and who are thus close to the source of goods. With her knowledge of English, Christina could surely get a job with the occupation forces. There's no future in tutoring other people's children, especially those of former Nazis, he warned Christina, who had just recently been employed by the Möller family. In their room on the second floor of the large white house belonging to the Director General of the local Engine Works Corporation, she tutored the children in German, English, and math, for which she earned a hundred marks a month, although, of course, there was nothing you could buy with it. But they treat her well, even provide her with a "second breakfast" as her pupils call it, toast and fruit, and sometimes even a piece of the chocolate that the Director receives as a gift in his dealings with the city's American Occupation Authority. Herr Möller is namely the one responsible for the restoration of local industrial operations, something Christina learns from his fifteen-year-old daughter Ellen. In the Möller household, there is a sense of hope, of planning for the future, of having survived the worst.

To Elise, in contrast, things look much bleaker. Her Philipp had risked his life for nothing, absolutely nothing. Bohrer, the informer, has already been released from custody and greeted her on the street so obsequiously as if nothing at all had happened. They've de-Nazified him, those Amis, thinking he had been no more than a sympathizer. It could not be proven that on several occasions Bohrer had informed against Philipp, since Herr Engel, the former mayor, had burned all the municipal records before he fled. It had all been for naught. The years of fear and anxiety, the sacrifices great and small. All in vain. Christina is at a loss to come up with anything to say to refute that. And yet she can't get out of her mind the word her father always used as his rallying cry, namely "Revolution," something that was inevitable if ever there were to be justice in this country. Her mother no longer believed in that. That whole idea had gotten lost.

Christina registers for school. Instruction takes place in a bunker in the city. On her way to school, Christina always goes past the Café Herder, which the Americans have turned into a Red Cross Club and whose entrance is guarded by Polish soldiers outfitted in American uniforms that have been dyed black. In the upper stories of the building, which had been damaged by bombing, German prisoners of war are clearing out the rubble. During recess, Christina sometimes sits on a pile of debris opposite the entrance and watches the comings and goings of the Americans. Once, one of the sentries tosses her a doughnut, the specialty of the Red Cross.

It was this doughnut that gave Christina the idea of applying for a job. The sentry gave her permission to go in through the back door to speak with the director of the club, a rather stout American woman in a blue uniform. With the help of her English dictionary, Christina had practiced introducing herself. She spoke slowly and made sure that she didn't mispronounce "th" like an "s". Miss Carlton thought Christina sufficiently talented to have her work at the information desk, where she would relieve the Red Cross women, who had more important things to do than show soldiers a map and tell them how to get from one place to another in this rubbish heap of a city. Christina didn't really care about being paid. What was important were the additional perks in the form of doughnuts and Coca-Colas and goodness knows what else.

The management of the club was in the capable hands of a Dutch man by the name of Alex. He ruled over the employees with absolute authority but was, thank heavens, friendly to the sole German employee under his command—because, as was later revealed, he had previously been an officer in the Waffen-SS. Christina did not have PX privileges like the non-German employees did, but people often gave her things. They looked the other way when she smuggled left-over doughnuts past the guards, hiding them under her new Ami sweater, and paid no mind when she regularly picked the longer cig-arette butts out of the ashtrays so she could roll new cigarettes out of them. These little operations presented no competition to the larger dealings the foreigners were engaged in. They, of course, were sitting close to the source—namely a warehouse full of cigarettes stamped "Not for Sale" that the Red Cross gave out to the soldiers, more than a few cartons of which found their way onto the black market.

Christina's shift was from three o'clock in the afternoon after school until ten at night, and if she missed the streetcar, sometimes she couldn't make it home before curfew. She would then creep along in the ditch next to the roadway to avoid being spotted by the patrol. If she suddenly saw a searchlight beam shining on the poplar trees that lined the road, she'd run through the high grass down to the river, holding up her skirt and carrying her shoes in her hand. She'd hide in a willow bush until the coast was clear again. Other than the fact that the big sandbar had shifted downstream, nothing had changed here. The well-worn footpath still snaked through the wild underbrush till it came to the "geese pasture," where Christina used to stand in the shallows and skip flat stones over the surface of the water. Even though she knew that the steep slope up to the sub-division was covered with stinging nettles, she took a chance and climbed up it anyway. In July, they don't sting, Tante Eva had al-ways claimed, but as it turned out, her aunt once again proved to be poorly informed.

If you keep falling for such old wives' tales, you've no right to complain, her mother said, as she dabbed a vinegar solution on the blisters that covered Christina's legs. Your Tante Eva, God rest her soul, would find this very funny if she could see you now! Eva's niece, however, started to wail for all she was worth, and Elise, surely not without sympathy, sat with her daughter at the kitchen table and cut up green beans for canning. The fact that rubber gaskets for canning jars were once again available was heartening to this housewife but failed to put a smile on Christina's glum face. What did cheer her up, though, was the fact that the bleeding heart she had planted on Tante Eva's grave was finally blooming.

With her legs stretched out on the footstool, Christina looked at her mother washing the canning jars and lids and stacking them on the dish rack to dry. She'll can the green beans early in the morning, but only after she has first hauled the heavy handcart from the central milk distribution center back to the branch outlet that the Heilemann Dairy operated in the subdivision, then unloaded all the milk cans. Her mother works there part-time and, in return, gets to keep whatever milk she can drain out of the cans before washing them. On good days that might be a liter or more of milk. The fact that she already walks somewhat bent over, and when standing, always has to put her hand on her back to keep herself from falling—this she attributes to heredity. Everybody has a cross to bear.

Not the Americans, says Christina. For instance, not Bill Treadway, a black giant of a man with gold-rimmed buck teeth. He plays boogie-woogie every day in the Red Cross Club's lounge. In the meantime, her mother has taken off her housecoat, rolled up her cotton undershirt, and is massaging her back with rubbing alcohol.

Then there's Jimmy Garfield—he's related to a president—he has studied history and has already read Felix Dahn's *Battle of Rome*, says the daughter who has all of a sudden become quite chatty with her mother. Do you already know them all by name? her mother asks. Just the regulars.

Christina is now supposed to rub alcohol on the places her mother can't reach, like her upper back. The Americans also smell good, Christina continues, and so that their German girlfriends will also smell good, they buy them Chanel No. 5 at the PX. That's perfume. Christina has to sneeze because of the fumes from the rubbing alcohol. To her mother's surprise, Christina wants to also give her a back rub. When she does, she suddenly notices how thin her mother has become. Like a washboard, exactly like a washboard. You can actually count her ribs through her skin.

The Americans are generous, Christina assures her mother, trying to say something to cheer her up. Her mother thinks they can well afford to be since they are the victors, and we're the vanquished. To tell from the photos they dug out of their wallets at every opportunity, they all have beautiful houses and big cars. That's why they want to go back home, says Christina. It would be just fine with her mother if they would all go right back where they came from.

And they do go back, but new ones come to replace them. They find their way around the city without any help from Christina. So she is transferred to the Commercial Cable Desk where she sends and receives telegrams, forwarding them to their respective recipients. The teletype machine is located in the basement, and Christina, who never learned how to type, tries doing it with just two fingers, which takes an eternity for her first telegram. Paris clatters back: Can you be quicker? Christina types: UNFORTUNATELY, NO! Jutta, her new colleague—a refugee from goodness knows where—understands the seriousness of the situation and gives Christina a crash course in typing. She had recommended Christina for the job, since she needed someone she could trust at this assignment. Here, everything is paid for in scrip, the currency of the American occupation forces, which is never supposed to fall into the wrong hands. It was only later—when Christina was too deeply involved to extricate herself from an awkward situation—that she realized that putting Jutta in charge of the Cable Desk was putting the fox in charge of the hen house.

Jutta didn't have a past, or at least she never spoke of it. But she spoke fluent Russian, Polish, and German. She had learned her English from the Americans, a mixture of jargon and street slang that she had picked up here and there and then dressed up with a dash of grammar. She was an original, she'd seen it all: indestructible, a person without scruples but with a big heart. In other words, someone made for these times.

Jutta lived in a garden shed somewhere on the edge of town, but since she found the club more congenial, she always stuck around a while after Christina had relieved her. Sometimes she waited for the fat corporal who handed her small packages, which she paid for with scrip. Usually it was just coffee, and she often shared a bit of it with Christina. One day, when she was going through the telegram forms, Christina figured out where Jutta got the scrip from. She shortened her customers' telegrams by eliminating any unnecessary words, and since they paid by the word, she made a little money on each telegram. The pennies slowly added up to dollars, and by the end of the week, she could place her order with the fat corporal. And so it happened that by Christmas, Christina also had scrip—enough to buy sugar and flour for making Christmas cookies. Jutta kept Christina's bad conscience in check by telling her about a certain Red Cross woman, a big operator who had managed to acquire, with help from Jutta, a very valuable painting in exchange for stolen cigarettes. We're still just little fish in this pond, Jutta kept saying, but she was on the lookout for bigger things.

Christina had to prepare for her final school examinations, though they didn't interest her in the least since she was not going to be able to attend the university anyway. She was not among the preferred candidates, unless an exception would be made for the daughters and sons of people who had been politically persecuted. But at this point Communists are distinctly out of favor, right? Onkel Werner, whom her mother had asked to once again exert his influence on his niece, thought she should be more careful about what she said. What does "be careful" mean? We have freedom of speech. We're living under American laws. And for that, replied Onkel Werner, we should be grateful. But what about the revolution? For this, her Onkel Werner had no answer and could only advise Christina to leave politics to those who knew what they were talking about. And just who is that supposed to be?

Christina did exceptionally well in history, German, and English. In the natural sciences, she didn't fare so well. But they made certain allowances for the first examinees after the war. In Christina's class in the bunker, for example, there were two classmates who had been visibly maimed by the war, one of whom had lost his right arm and could only be examined orally. Everybody passed, and the party they had to celebrate the occasion turned into a veritable eating orgy, thanks to the doughnuts that Christina had been saving up for the whole previous week.

So, you've got your diploma, the postal inspector said. He had come to oversee the orderly takeover of the Cable Desk by the German Post Office. Jutta, who had refused to provide her personal background information, was summarily dismissed. Christina took her place and officially became a civil servant. Imagine that! Jutta was not unhappy to finally get out of there, since under the watchful eyes of the German Post Office her dealings would not run as smoothly as before. Besides, at the moment she was in negotiations with a man from Switzerland who was looking for an agent here in the American zone. The Americans were in the process of selling off military vehicles, and these could only be purchased by one of the Allies. The Swiss, whose German clients needed some Jeeps, would order them from Paris, while Jutta would do whatever was necessary to have them delivered to the Germans. This is the big time, no kidding! You'd be amazed!

Christina's admiration of Jutta's ingenuity knew no bounds. The way she so casually raked her fingers through her short salt-and-pepper hair, slipped into her American overcoat, and marched through the main entrance, breaking all the rules— she was the epitome of audacity. She was just as audacious when, dressed like a farmhand, she hoed her way across the border through a potato field and disappeared into Switzerland without a trace.

Anxiety about the upcoming winter begins already in the fall. This winter can't possibly be worse than the last one at the end of the war, but you still have to make sure you have something to burn for heat. The Americans have cleared the forest at Blumenau, but you can apply for a permit from the mayor's office that will allow you to dig up a tree stump. With permit in hand and an axe and spade in a handcart, Christina and her mother set out. This is not a job for women, says the man who is kind enough to tell them how to deal with the long tree roots. When, after many hours of work, they have gotten the stump out of the ground, they are missing the wedge they need to split the wood. But the stump couldn't just be left lying there, since it would be gone by morning for sure. So Christina keeps watch until it gets completely dark, and early the next morning, they come back to finish the job. Christina's hands, not used to such heavy labor, are bleeding through her gloves. This is torture, she complains, I'm not doing this anymore. And so, the next night she and Gerda dismantle the wooden barricade that the Americans have put up on the road leading to the blown-up bridge over the canal.

Before long, a patrol jeep comes driving up the road, but fortunately stops just short of the single plank that the two of them had thoughtfully left lying across the road. How's that for luck! You can say that again, chuckled Gerda, as she helped Christina cover the stolen wood with a tarp. *And that is only our first strike, the next will come another night!* No sooner had the Americans put up another barricade than it was taken down overnight, until the Amis decided they needed to build a temporary bridge. In order to do that, they'd have to blow up what was left of the old bridge, part of which was under water. And when you set off explosives under water, there will be enough dead fish to feed the whole village—this according to Fritz Nagel, the former Pioneer. So, the idea was to jump into the water with fish nets in hand right after they set off the explosion. What Fritz failed to mention was that the fish would, for the most part, only be stunned and gasping for air. After diving in headfirst, Christina came to the surface and saw nothing but flapping and thrashing fish swimming all around her. She felt like the boy in the fairy tale who had set out into the world to experience fear.[18] With great effort she managed to swim through the sea of fish to the motorboat of the American detonation squad, who had already hauled out of the water several others who had experienced the gruesome scene. Gerda, who had done her fishing from the shore, was happy to share her catch, but by that point Christina had completely lost her appetite for fish— whether baked, fried, or pickled.

All expectations to the contrary, the first post-war winter turned out to be the most miserable yet. Driven by hunger, every weekend Christina and Gerda scoured the countryside for food, convinced that somewhere there must be some farmer who needed a suit, or whose wife couldn't resist her desire to own a collection of Rosenthal demitasse cups.

Spring was even more miserable, even though the holes that the war had made in the family were slowly being filled back in. Maybe for that reason the absences that remained were all the more painful.

---

[18] A reference to one of the Grimms' fairy tales, *Von einem, der auszog, das Fürchten zu lernen* (About someone who went out into the world to learn about fear).

Tante Anna's eldest, Karl, returned from imprisonment in Canada well fed and fluent in English. Her George was released from Russian captivity with a kidney infection, his body covered with boils. The British had also released Tante Eva's Heinz, who seemed almost more upset by Germany's defeat than by the death of his foster mother. He grieved about his lost career in the military, since now he'd have to start all over in his old trade as a mason. He was even so bold as to suggest to his Tante Elise that she should turn over to him the construction company, and with it the motorcycle that belonged to her missing husband. Elise took umbrage at the fact that the family already considered Philipp to be lost. It was not yet that final. The Red Cross was still looking for him. It would indeed keep looking, until thirty years later, it would report to her that most likely her husband had been killed in the early days of February 1945, one of the countless casualties of his unit's involvement in the scorched earth retreat from Kulm on the Weichsel. This was at precisely the same time that he had been home or leave from the front....

Innocent of this post-war Red Cross report, back in the spring of '46 Elise still had reason to hope.

On the other hand, Christina, who had gotten in touch with a few of her father's comrades-in-suffering, among them Fritz Bertold from Sandhausen, thought differently. Since the revolution they'd planned had to be foresworn, most of these comrades had been murdered shortly before the end of the war. And that was fine with their fellow countrymen who had skeletons in their own closets, just as it was for the Americans, who had even less sympathy for the Communists than for the Nazis. Philipp was never coming home. At least he was spared the realization that it had all been in vain. Christina found it hard to believe that her father would have taken it all as calmly as did Herr Bertold.

Christina was convinced, for example, that her father would have done something about his competitor in the neighboring vil-

lage, the super-patriot August Stein. It was this very same Nazi
Party member Stein who—Christina was sure her mother must remember this—had managed, through various means of chicanery,
to steal customers from her father. How could anyone contract with
a builder when you never knew when he might land in jail again?
This is what Stein had purportedly said to Herr Voss, who sub-
sequently cancelled his contract with Philipp to build Voss's new
house. Just so you know! You only know that from hearsay, claimed
Tante Lisa, who thought it her duty to defend Herr Stein, since she
had just had him repair her roof. No one in the group agreed with
Christina, although they were all celebrating Tante Lisa's birthday
today with the coffee Christina had provided, and thus might have
shown her a little gratitude. No, Christina, you don't really know
your father. Tante Lisa insists that she never considered Philipp a
vengeful person. Even Tante Klara, now in a relationship with an
extremely competent black marketeer and therefore already the
owner of a small house under construction, was of the opinion that
one should let sleeping dogs lie. Philipp was never one to carry a
grudge. He, too, would be happy that it's all over with.

Not only is it all over with, but things are actually getting better—
this according to the Red Cross field director. Mr. Carey had come
to the occupation zone to provide comfort and advice to Americans
in emotional distress. And whenever he had free time, which he
seemed to have quite often, he also liked to busy himself with the
emotional burdens of the Germans. He was the only person who was
willing to discuss the events of the past with Christina. He wanted
to hear from her exactly what it had been like. Sometimes, he even
took notes. It was only when the term "Communist" was mentioned
that he would pause and sort of shrug. But he'd sit up straight and
with arms outstretched talk excitedly about democracy and the in-
alienable rights of his republic, rights that would soon be introduced

in this country as well. Then there will be justice, he assured Christina. Then things will be different.

But in an effort to do something nice for Christina right now, he would sometimes engage her as an interpreter—for money, of course. Mostly that happened when he faced the unpleasant task of convincing German women not to get involved in a mixed marriage with a black soldier. It was not easy to get the idea across in German to these women that such a marriage would not be accepted by white Americans. But why exactly? Mr. Carey would then put on his glasses and shuffle through the papers on his desk, as if he might find the answer written there. He wanted only the best for those concerned, who would then slowly get up from their seats, a white hand holding a black one, and leave. It's an awkward situation, Miss Christina, hard for foreigners to understand.

The so-called rubble flowers were blooming for a second time. For centuries they had supposedly lain dormant under the city until debris and ashes, their preferred fertilizer, had enabled them to re-emerge. An American in civilian clothing admired the yellow blossoms that Christina had stuck in a Coca-Cola bottle on her desk. He would like to pick up a telegram that had come through for him yesterday by telephone. Mr. Morey, of course! Christina smiled as she handed him the envelope. She remembered the signature—"Love and million kisses, Kitty"—which she had had to repeat twice over the phone because the recipient had not heard her correctly.

He has dark brown hair and steel blue eyes. He offers her a cigarette from a gold cigarette case, which she accepts with thanks but slips into her desk drawer. He asks her if she'd like something to eat. He seems not to know the house rules. Whatever is on offer upstairs in the canteen is only for the Americans. That can't be true, he says, and disappears up the stairs. After a few minutes, he comes back with a tray full of food, puts it down on Christina's desk, and leaves. Christina eats the soft roll first. Then she uses a telegram form to wrap the ground meat patty with cheese melted on top to save for later, since she can't imagine eating it without a knife and fork. She hesitantly sucks the milky drink in the glass up through the straw. She doesn't care for milk, but this is not really milk—it's liquid vanilla ice cream. A milkshake, Miss Lawrence calls it. She has suddenly appeared in front of Christina's desk but pretends not to notice that Christina is not following the rules.

Some Americans aren't really so bad, Christina assures her classmates who, for old times' sake, have gotten together at Peter Schmidt's house. Peter, who had been drafted into the civil defense corps and imprisoned by the Americans and, as a result, had suffered—or so he implied—various indignities, tries to avoid Americans whenever possible. He therefore finds it very unfortunate that Christina has to associate with them every day. Hans Paul agrees with him. He himself always sticks to the side streets when walking through the city, because one evening two drunk American soldiers had cursed him and blocked his way.

Christina was surprised that Hans was still around, given that the humiliating defeat of the Germans which he had sworn he would never survive had, in fact, occurred. But there he sits opposite her with his legs spread wide, his long torso leaning over the tiled table on which Frau Schmidt is placing a carafe of raspberry juice right under his chin. Soda water and glasses are set out on the tea cart. Hans asks his hostess for an ashtray. He's recently started smoking, thereby abusing the Aryan body that he had kept pure all those years through strict abstinence and constant exercise. He had dedicated himself wholeheartedly to the Führer, and by virtue of such total devotion had once gone so far as to denounce Christina to the school principal because of some politically questionable remarks she had made in class. What she had done was tell a story about a woman who, unable to buy butter at the weekly market, in her anger, reportedly said for all to hear that she'd just spit in the frying pan and say "Heil Hitler"—that would be just as greasy. After Christina had been called to the principal's office and given a very stern talking-to, she punished Hans for weeks by giving him the silent treatment.

Hans still cannot understand how the Americans could have won the war. Erich Bauer knows how but indicates with a dismissive gesture that he doesn't want to waste his breath talking about it. Gudrun agrees with him, since she finds the whole conversation incredibly boring. Besides, she has nothing against the Americans. We should just be glad it's all over. Everybody *is* glad, says Jürgen Winter, who has finally managed to get accepted to study at the university, even though he had done very poorly on his exams. Of course, he has his father to thank for that, since his father was a member and former standard-bearer of two dueling fraternities, and had moved heaven and earth to make it possible for his son to study law at the university.

Jürgen finds it odd that Christina doesn't want to go on to the university, since she had always gotten good grades. We sure hope our model German girl won't get involved with an American, Hans says, with something like a threat hidden in his comment.

No, she won't. She goes to dancing class at the Kneisebeck dance studio and tangos with Walter Zehler, letting him pull her up from the deep dips of the dance and hold her close to his chest. Walter has also managed to survive the war and has now fully dedicated himself to re-building Germany. He wants to become an architect, and Christina has loaned him her drawing board and materials, even her protractor and T-square. That's why he often drops by, and Christina's mother, who finds him quite likable, secretly hopes that something might come of the relationship. But Christina also sometimes gets together with Volker Zahn, who had been in her class in the bunker and who is a theatre fan. He particularly likes Lessing, whose play *Nathan the Wise* has been running for several months in the Schauburg, an old movie theater whose stage has been temporarily modified to accommodate theatre performances. Pretty soon the two of them know the play by heart, since they have seen it three times. The concept of "tolerance," picked up from Lessing's play and the subject of lively discussions with Volker on their walks through the fields and woods, becomes Christina's motto. It comes up, for example, as soon as her mother begins making insulting comments about her daughter's relationship with a certain Dieter from God knows where. Dieter is a refugee, and refugees are suspect. They all claim to have been wealthy, her mother says, and now they want restitution from us. Somebody else might buy his sob story about his parents having had an estate in Pomerania, but not Elise. She prefers Robert Hähnle, even though he is not from around here either. There is a flurry of letter-writing going on between Robert and Christina. He had been one of the prisoners of war who worked on the labor detail clearing rubble out of the Red Cross Club, and Christina had supplied him with doughnuts and then visited him in the prisoners' camp. He's now living in the French occupation zone, and it takes months before she can get a pass to go visit him there. He's still cramming for his final exams, and she quizzes him on his Latin vocabulary—for which he thanks her with a kiss. Robert comes from a large family. The two younger daughters have already been married off, for which the family is grateful, particularly since one of them is the wife of a farmer and thus provides the family with food. Before you eat at the Hähnles, you have to pray and make the sign of the cross. The eldest daughter, whose eyes during the blessing gaze fervently at the crucifix hanging on the wall behind the dining banquette, works at the post office and is financing her younger brother's education. Robert is the youngest.

Following the death of the father, the eldest son, a teacher, is now the head of the family. He is the one who cross-examines Christina, since Robert seems to be seriously infatuated with her. Would she be prepared to convert to Catholicism? When he asks this question, Christina can only think of the smell of incense, which had almost knocked her over when, early in the morning and on an empty stomach, she had knelt next to Robert in the convent church. She'll need to think that over, she says. All of a sudden, she also needs to leave, which makes Robert very sad. The kiss at the train station is something that she won't forget for a long time. And Robert apparently doesn't either, since he writes to say that he loves her. Christina sends him a package of Butterfingers and cigarettes. He writes her that he loves her very much. She writes him about the dancing class graduation ball and the fancy dress that Tante Lisa had made for her for this special occasion from some old, light brown damask drapes. Christina's ever so graceful moves on the dance floor caused this material, which had been hanging for years in Tante Lisa's parlor absorbing the smoke of countless cigars and cigarettes, to give off such a stench that even Christina could no longer stand it, so she just took off, leaving Walter without a dance partner. She does not write Robert that the Americans conducted a raid that night, and that she, in possession of both scrip and cigarettes, had spent half the night sitting in the MP station, along with the other black marketeers, awaiting the threatened interrogation. The salmon-colored rose that Tante Lisa had tucked into her décolletage—the neckline of her dress having ended up exposing more than intended—was already wilted by the time the sergeant called her into the hearing room. The fact that she works for the Americans is no excuse. The young lieutenant hands her a piece of paper showing the address where she is to appear the following morning. It's because of the scrip: it had been issued just the week before and had already fallen into the wrong hands. That's a matter for the Criminal Investigation Division, where Christina presents herself the next morning.

Fortunately, the investigating officer is Mr. Morey, who very politely offers her a chair. Love and million kisses, says Christina, and he laughs and asks his secretary, who is sitting there ready to take notes, to leave him alone with the young lady. The only way she can get out of this mess is to accept his invitation to go to a party with him. Christina would later contend that she had thought this over for a long time. But she hadn't. He would have his driver pick her up at the back door of the club after work.

The party was in the apartment of an American couple, the Topes, both of whom worked for the government and were old friends of Matt Morey. For dinner there were beans and bacon in a sweet sauce, and ham. The ham stood in all its round, juicy glory on a platter in front of Henry Tope, who carved as much as the guests wanted. If you wanted a second helping, you just needed to nod in the affirmative in response to Henry's questioning glance. Accompanying the main course, there were square slices of bread that almost tasted like cake. Just not quite as sweet, Christina thought, after she had conducted several taste tests.

The other guests were officers with their wives or girlfriends, who ate very little but drank quite a bit of whiskey and more or less ignored Christina on this particular evening. That was fine with her, since it was very strenuous trying to figure out what they were saying. After a few unsuccessful attempts to participate in the conversation, she decided to devote her full attention to the meal. The Topes couldn't believe how much this slight German girl could put away. The invited guests became friendlier to Christina only when, under the influence of the whisky, they seemed to forget that she was a German. They suddenly found her accent charming and seemed willing to overlook her outfit, which consisted of a hodge-podge of articles of American army clothing. When they were leaving, Matt even had to promise to bring Christina along to the Officers Club, to a cocktail party which was being arranged for the following Friday in honor of Matt. It was his birthday.

For the occasion, Christina wore the blouse made of parachute silk, by far the best thing in her wardrobe, even though it had yellow circles under the arms from perspiration because the fabric was not at all breathable. Her skirt, made from the trousers of an American officer's uniform, had wide kick pleats in front and back, so she could hike it up and it wouldn't get dirty when she walked through tall grass. The American women came dressed in the latest New Look, decked out in ankle-length skirts and blouses with plunging necklines, teetering on high heels that made it hard for them to walk. Christina, on the other hand, clomping up the marble steps of the Officers Club in her wooden clogs with Matt at her side, was standing on firm footing when, at the top of the stairs, an American woman came up to her and let her have it. "Damned Nazi-Kraut," she snarled through her cherry-red lips. Those sitting inside on low chairs around small tables craned their necks to look through the doorway to where Christina stood as if rooted, where she had to watch Matt take the tottering blonde by the arm and steer her over to the bar, most likely in an effort to remove her from harm's way. Maggie Tope, carefully balancing her martini glass with its olive on a toothpick in her right hand, guided Christina with her left toward the Ladies Room where they could talk about this in private. That was Kitty, Kitty Landon, a former girlfriend of Matt's, Maggie explained, as she raised her pencil-thin arched eyebrows and then lowered them again as Christina nodded her head in understanding.

Maggie decided she also wanted to use the toilet, and although, to Christina's amazement, she left the stall door open, her words were lost in the sound of her peeing and the subsequent flushing. From her seated vantage point, Maggie must have noticed Christina's shoes. They were two rounded, foot-shaped pieces of wood with black leather laces. With each step, her toes had to curl down to grasp the front of the clog, while the rear part sounded clip-clop as its metal heel tap slapped the tile floor.

When, a week later, Matt appeared again at the Cable Desk, he handed Christina a package from Maggie. In it was a pair of high-heeled patent-leather pumps. Although she tried with all her might to force her wide feet into the narrow shoes, it just wouldn't work. She wanted to keep them nevertheless—they were prime material for bartering on the black market. In the meantime, she stuck the shoes in her desk, where her mother wouldn't see them, since she had already grown suspicious about why Christina had recently had to work late so many evenings. Don't get involved with an American, for God's sake, not an American, she said. With the likes of them, you'll lose your reputation!

Christina wanted to keep her good reputation. She always had Matt drop her off when they got to the bridge so that no one living on the upper end of August-Bebelstrasse—formerly Hindenburg-strasse—would notice that someone was being brought home in a Jeep. She always stayed on the bridge for a few minutes until the Jeep had turned around at the foot of the bridge and headed back toward the city.

You should think about where things go from here, Matt suggested one night, as Christina unwound herself from the white army blanket that always lay there for her on the seat of the Jeep, since even though it was just the beginning of fall, she was always shivering. Matt seemed to know what he wanted. He was serious about Christina, and he wanted to declare his intentions to her family. Christina also knew what she wanted, and that was a winter coat. If

Matt had been paying closer attention, he would have noticed how often Christina gazed longingly at the white woolen blanket and how sad she was to leave it lying next to its owner, who then just tossed it into the back seat of the Jeep when they parted each evening.

From the bridge, Christina can see into Gerda's attic room if she has the window open. Ever since Gerda's father had taken up with a refugee woman, Gerda had had to go back to sleeping in the attic. The plywood partition that her father had put up in his bedroom, so that his daughter would have her own little alcove to sleep in, had now been taken down.

Beautiful Helene, as Gerda called her father's new girlfriend, was jealous of Gerda and wanted to get her out of the house. The Bohrers, who had previously been using the small room in the attic for storage, didn't want to rent it out any longer—after all, they were the property owners and could decide how to use the space. For the rent that Gerda's father Fritz paid, he'd never find a two-bedroom apartment anywhere in the village, not even a stable or a chicken coop, is what Frau Bohrer supposedly screamed down the stairwell to him. And besides, she didn't want any whoring going on in her house! In the past, Fritz would have simply let that accusation pass without comment.

But not these days. Thus it had come to the first public political argument, which spread beyond the Bohrer's yard all the way down the street, offering the neighbors who came running out of curiosity the opportunity to declare their true colors. The rule of the Brownshirts is over, yelled Red Commie Fritz, and since there were no barricades around, he planted himself on top of the sand pile that had been dumped in front of the entrance to the Späther's yard for repairing the stucco on their house. It's high time we made things clear around here. You don't have to put up with the likes of them, he shouted, all the while pointing his finger at Frau Bohrer. Christina burst out with the words to the popular Socialist anthem *Brothers to the sun, to freedom, brothers to the light*, but there were not enough voices to form a chorus, since other than Christina and her mother, who did not join in, nobody seemed to know the words to the song. She would gladly have sung the second verse as well, but the neighbors had slowly drifted away, and Fritz had taken off after Frau Bohrer, who had already fled into her house before Christina could continue her serenade to freedom.

Frau Bohrer let Fritz keep the attic room, but only, she explained to Frau Späther, in order to keep the peace. Frau Späther, who has also been forced to take in refugees, could sympathize with Frau Bohrer's predicament. So, it's come to this, has it? We're no longer in control of our own property, lamented Frau Späther, as she shoveled her sand back onto the pile that had been trampled down.

On this cool fall evening, there is still a light on in the attic room, and Christina, who for some time had been observing her surroundings while deep in thought, decides to go see Gerda. But in order to get up to the attic, she has to knock on Fritz's door. He grumpily hands the door key to her through the bedroom window. She apologizes for disturbing him.

Christina hurries up the stairs and is out of breath when she reaches Gerda's door. Gerda was just about to go to bed because she has to get up early the next morning. She is back working at the Fulmina factory, where they'd changed over from making replacement parts for tanks to making pots and kitchen utensils. Gerda now has a steady boyfriend, but he's not allowed to come to the house. Helene won't allow it, and Gerda's father is very obedient to his beautiful girlfriend. Christina has it better since Robert would be allowed to visit her if he could. But Gerda knows that Christina is secretly dating an American and is therefore enmeshed in a web of white lies that she can't find a way out of. Gerda does not envy Christina that.

He wants to marry me, this American. Christina winces as she utters this statement, as though someone else has made it in order to frighten her. Gerda's face registers both surprise and dismay. For the first time, she is unable to find anything humorous to say in a predicament. Gerda is speechless. Things are getting serious.

Just before midnight, Christina lets herself into the house and tiptoes up the creaky stairs to her room, where her mother is sitting on Christina's bed, her hands in her lap, twiddling her thumbs. That Ami, she says, will not be allowed in this house.

Early in the winter, Christina gets sick. Her chronic shivering is followed by a chronic cough. Miss Day, the Red Cross Club's new director and a trained nurse, worries that Christina might be infectious. You can never tell what sort of germs these natives might be carrying around, given the state of their nutrition.

Miklos, Miss Day's driver, has to take Christina to the American military clinic to be examined. The doctor presses his ice-cold stethoscope to her chest and back while she breathes in and out. He looks in her throat and ears. His face gives off a sickeningly sweet smell so that Christina has to hold her breath until he's out of range. He coughs as though a bit embarrassed, as though he doesn't know exactly how to proceed. He then explains to her, very slowly and deliberately, that when examining German girls and women, he is obligated to take a swab to test for any indication of venereal disease. Not until he shortens the name of the disease to the two initials she recognizes, namely VD, does Christina figure out what he's about to do. She searches for words but can't come up with any in English that are appropriate to this situation. Her native tongue, however, is up to the challenge. The doctor, lacking any knowledge of German but in an officious manner meant to demonstrate his superiority, has meanwhile gone and sat down at his desk and is writing notes with his left hand while seeming to form the letters with his mouth. And since he's obviously not bright enough to know who he's dealing with, Christina gathers up her clothes and marches into the anteroom, where the note writer stares at her, goggle-eyed, as she gets dressed.

She waits in the Jeep for Miklos who, as instructed by Miss Day, had remained in the waiting room for the results of the exam, and who has heard about the entire episode from the doctor himself. It was only when Miklos put his arm around her shoulder and gave her a hug that Christina had to pull herself together so as not to lose her composure. It's only a low-grade lung infection, Miklos said, handing her a white envelope with the pills the doctor had given him. One, three times a day, and at the very least one week of bed rest. He'll drive her home.

Because Elise had injured her back and could no longer lift the milk cans, she is now helping out behind the counter at the milk store, a vantage point from which she has an unobstructed view of the approach to the bridge. She sees the Jeep turn into the subdivision and recognizes the passenger. Contrary to her normal behavior, she leaves the store full of customers and rushes home, where her daughter is already heating water for linden blossom tea and assures her mother that it's nothing serious. Only a cold.

When the next Jeep drives up to the house a few days later and a stranger—to all appearances an American—greets Frau Späther, who as usual is leaning out of her window, Elise's heart is in her throat. So, it's come to this.

When the doorbell rings, she takes off her apron and arranges her freshly waved hair. She takes her time. Only after the bell rings a second time does she open the door. The man inquiring about Miss Christina is older than she had expected. His German is terrible, but he seems to understand everything. No, he may not talk to Christina. She's lying down. Elise takes the small package wrapped with blue ribbon and promises to give it to the patient. Along with his greetings, of course, with his greetings! Mr. Morey. He will return. On Sunday. He shakes her hand.

He's much too delicately built for a man. And his hands, Lisa, they're so finely shaped and manicured, clearly he doesn't earn his living with them. I bet you he must be at least thirty.

Elise could tell that his intentions were serious.

Tante Lisa had come over on Sunday to represent the family's interests since, after all, you can't let the girl be taken across the ocean by just anybody. Tante Lisa can read people. You can't put anything over on her. She'll give this Ami a thorough going over.

In the living room, which has been heated for this special occasion, two candles are burning on the advent wreath that has been placed on a crystal platter in the middle of the round oak table. Christina's mother once again straightens the lace tablecloth that she had crocheted herself. Christina is standing by the window looking at the driving snow. Maybe he won't come in this weather, she says. Ach, the snow is melting as soon as it hits the ground. He'll come.

You've already met my mother. And this is Tante Lisa. He's brought a bottle of cognac, among other things, and Elise takes the brandy glasses out of the buffet and pours. Matt offers the ladies cigarettes, and Tante Lisa accepts. They talk about the weather. Much too early for snow. Does it snow where you come from? Not much in California, just sometimes in the mountains. Does he have a family? Yes, two brothers and one sister. Matt looks over at Christina, who is still standing by the window and looking out at the street. Tante Lisa wants to know what he does, that is, what kind of work. He's a lawyer, at the moment serving as a first lieutenant in the Army's Criminal Investigation Division, but in the CID, all the investigators wear civilian clothes. Really! You don't say! That must be nice, not to have a wear a uniform. Don't you think so, Elise?

Christina's mother looks at him in silence. Somewhat embarrassed, he takes a box of cookies out of his briefcase, and chocolates, and coffee, as well as a small package. Oh, that's really not necessary, she says, blushing like a school girl. You'd think it was Christmas, she says, while she opens the package. With a silk scarf patterned with colorful flowers and a bottle of Chanel No. 5, one can work wonders. Besides, there's something irresistible about this man, Tante Lisa would later remark, and Elise thought so as well.

Elise asks him whether he understands that one doesn't want to lose one's only child. He does understand, but she can come and join her daughter later. She is still waiting for her husband to return. While Christina's mother—who has become quite talkative from the cognac—shares with this stranger the details of her unfortunate situation, Matt and Tante Lisa try to out-smoke each other.

Christina, who feels completely superfluous to this scene, slips unnoticed out of the room into the yard and then into the street, where she takes the white woolen Ami blanket out of Matt's Jeep and wraps herself in it. Then she goes back into the house and stuffs the blanket into her wardrobe. By the time she comes back in, Tante Lisa and Matt are already addressing each other in the familiar "du" form, because Matt can't keep the "du" and "Sie" forms straight anyway, which Tante Lisa points out to him, playfully threatening him with her index finger. Matt is invited to come for Christmas. Tante Lisa gets her hand kissed, Elise gets a half-hug, and Christina gets his assurance that everything is okay now.

Christina has the blanket dyed light blue and has a coat made out of it. A cape really, without buttons, according to the latest fashion. Robert, who comes unannounced to visit shortly before Christmas, finds the cape very chic. Her mother thinks it should have been lined because of the printing on the inside. She also thinks that Christina ought to come clean with Robert. Christina wanted to but just couldn't find the right moment. She didn't have the heart to spoil his happiness about being admitted to medical school. Only when she grabbed Robert's hand through the train window to say goodbye did the time seem right. But all she said was "Take care of yourself" instead of "Auf Wiedersehen," as if that settled everything.

In order to make marriage between an American citizen and an enemy alien as complicated as possible, the military government required a dossier, the assembly of which tripped up many an applicant. But by virtue of his position, Matt had connections. He personally carried the documents from one office to the next. The CID had some concerns because the applicant had purportedly made comments that could be interpreted as politically suspect. Besides, she was the daughter of a former Communist cell leader. In order to marry, CID Officer Matthew Morey would have to give up his top-secret security clearance. He must have anguished considerably before deciding to make this sacrifice, since he didn't come around for weeks, something that Christina didn't seem to hold against him. In response to her mother's question as to whether she actually loved him, Christina only nodded her head. Does she want to, or doesn't she? She should think it over once again, very seriously, because she can still change her mind. Christina didn't change her mind. When, after returning from an assignment in France, Matt's request to be released from active duty was approved, there was nothing further standing in the way of the wedding.

It took place on the Fourth of July, and the village residents thought the huge fireworks display that the Americans set off in the city was in honor of the newlyweds. Two weeks later Christina stood at the railing of the *Blanche F. Sigman*, throwing flowers over the side, flowers that then floated on the waves back toward Bremerhaven. A gust of wind lifted up her light blue cape, revealing on the unlined inside, in large black letters, US PROPERTY.

The curve of the Neckar enclosing the village (Ilvesheim)

(From the American Geographical Society Library, University of Wisconsin-Milwaukee /
©Stadt Mannheim, Fachbereich Geoinformation und Vermessung)

Philipp in his early twenties, at the beginning of his career as architect and builder

The author, seated, second row from front (in horizontally-striped top)

Father and daughter setting off on the motorcycle trip

The author, 3rd from left; her mother, 4th from left; her father, 3rd from right

The straw hat that convinced the author's daughter that her mother was not a Nazi:
"Nazis didn't wear . . . straw hats. . . ."

The author, about age seventeen

The Neckar canal with barge traffic; in the background, houses in the "new" subdivision

Philipp in uniform in Russia, 1944

After the July 4, 1948 wedding ceremony

The new bride and groom. Elise on the author's right, Matt (in suit) and his best man

162

Leaving Bremerhaven for New York on the Blanche F. Sigman

Afterword

As suggested initially, my mother's extended wrestling with her subject—putting down on paper this account of her life up to her departure from her "fatherland"—was likely a process by which she sought to come to terms with her rather traumatic past. The narrative would, as well, allow her to explore the foundation that had determined her youth and on which she built her American life.

The preceding account of my mother's parental and familial relationships brings into focus the complex psychology of a young girl growing up during a period of political and social upheaval. In particular, she tries to articulate what it meant to be the daughter of an avowed Communist who was actively opposed to the Hitler regime, and whose political convictions put his own—and his family's—existence at risk, since he was frequently taken into custody and imprisoned during the Nazi era. She provides insight as to what it was like to be the daughter of a political activist who was conscripted into military service very late in the war, only to disappear under dubious circumstances—the belated, official explanation for which she never accepted.

My mother's memoir closes with her about to embark upon a new life in the United States, leaving family and familiarity—and perhaps some untamed demons—behind. What lay ahead after that portentous sailing from Bremerhaven was unknown to the new bride who had just recently become the "property" of the United States.

As her daughter, I can assure the reader that "Christina" lived a full and rewarding life as an American citizen. Her marriage to my father, Matthew Moore, ended in a separation in the 1970s, although they never divorced. My father died in 1978, many years after having retired from the US Army Criminal Investigation Division (CID) with the rank of Major. I was their only child. As predicted in the memoir, my grandmother—the story's "Elise"—joined her daughter and American son-in-law in the US in the early 1950s and lived with us for many years before eventually returning to Germany and remarrying.

In the 1960s, my mother was at last able to pursue a college education in the United States, an opportunity she, like so many other women, did not have in Germany at the end of the war. She ultimately completed her bachelor's, master's, and doctoral degrees and enjoyed a distinguished, decades-long career as a beloved educator at a midwestern university. In 1993, full of enthusiasm for a future that was still unfolding, she entered into a second marriage with Lee Baxandall, an American writer and activist. She was widowed a second time upon his death in 2008.

Johanna Christina Barbara Steigleder Moore Baxandall died in 2017 at the age of eighty-nine. Her memoir was discovered some months later.

Acknowledgments

The translators give special thanks to Carolyn Sonneborn Mayr, whose translation assistance and overall support of this project was invaluable. We also thank the many friends and colleagues who made time to review the several early and imperfect drafts of the translation, or who otherwise offered helpful advice. These include: Peetie Basson, Phineas Baxandall, John Buntin, Linda Buntin, Dot Glover, John Hanson, Sarah Hill, Leone Lewensohn, Edith Moravczik, Thomas Schleissing-Niggemann, John Surber, and Ned Weckmueller. Their comments and suggestions were critical to our efforts to remain faithful to the writer's original language and style while transforming both into what we wanted to be an engaging version in English.

And finally, the translators' thanks to the author's son-in-law, John Steen, who discovered the typescript and brought it to our attention. He was unwavering in his encouragement and support of this project.